MAINE DOINGS

by

Robert P. Tristram Coffin

with decorations by the author

THE BOBBS-MERRILL COMPANY, INC.

INDIANAPOLIS   *Publishers*   NEW YORK

MAINE DOINGS

Books by

ROBERT P. TRISTRAM COFFIN

POEMS

CHRISTCHURCH
DEW AND BRONZE
GOLDEN FALCON
THE YOKE OF THUNDER
BALLADS OF SQUARE-TOED AMERICANS
STRANGE HOLINESS
SALTWATER FARM
MAINE BALLADS

COLLECTED POEMS
THERE WILL BE BREAD AND LOVE
PRIMER FOR AMERICA
POEMS FOR A SON WITH WINGS
PEOPLE BEHAVE LIKE BALLADS
COLLECTED POEMS, NEW AND
    ENLARGED EDITION
ONE-HORSE FARM

ESSAYS

BOOK OF CROWNS AND COTTAGES
AN ATTIC ROOM
CHRISTMAS IN MAINE
BOOK OF UNCLES

MAINSTAYS OF MAINE
YANKEE COAST
COAST CALENDAR
MAINE DOINGS

BIOGRAPHIES

LAUD: STORM CENTER OF STUART ENGLAND
THE DUKES OF BUCKINGHAM
PORTRAIT OF AN AMERICAN (*The Author's Father*)
CAPTAIN ABBY AND CAPTAIN JOHN (*Abby and John Pennell,*
    Brunswick, Maine)

AUTOBIOGRAPHY

LOST PARADISE (*The Author's Life to His Twelfth Year*)

NOVELS

RED SKY IN THE MORNING
JOHN DAWN
THOMAS-THOMAS-ANCIL-THOMAS

LECTURES

NEW POETRY OF NEW ENGLAND (*Frost and Robinson*)
    (*The Turnbull Memorial Lectures,* Johns Hopkins University)
THE SUBSTANCE THAT IS POETRY
    (*The Patten Lectures,* Indiana University)
THE THIRD HUNGER & THE POEM ALOUD
    (*The Samuel Harris Lectures,* Bangor Theological Seminary)
    (*Speech Club Lecture,* Texas State College for Women)

HISTORY

KENNEBEC: CRADLE OF AMERICANS
    (*The Rivers of America Series*)

TEXTS

A BOOK OF SEVENTEENTH-CENTURY PROSE
SEVENTEENTH-CENTURY PROSE AND POETRY
    (*Both with A. M. Witherspoon*)

To

JUNIPER

MY SPARKLING STATE-OF-MAINE GOD-DAUGHTER

and

ALL THE OTHER SPARKLING BERKELEYS

JIM

NELL

MERCY

ACKNOWLEDGMENT

THE author is grateful to the editors of several periodicals and the editors of the Writers' War Board for their permission to reprint materials which first appeared under their hands; among the periodicals are: *The American Mercury, The Christian Science Monitor, Gourmet,* and *The Reader's Digest.*

Contents

I

MAINE
GOINGS-ON

1. The Jenny Lind Dollar

MY FATHER was a man fairly well-off, for the little Yankee town we lived in. Anyway, he left all of us children a house or so apiece.

Once when I was thigh-high to a grasshopper and had earned a whole quarter of a dollar picking potato-bugs off our potatoes at five cents a cupful, my father took me on his wide knee and told me how he earned his first dollar.

[11]

Father was a small boy then, no bigger than I was that potato-bug day. But he wore trousers down to his ankles, for that was a long time ago, just a little after they discovered gold in California. Father, with his short legs, had no hope of getting as far as California and the gold. But something more exciting than all the ore of the Pacific Coast was going to be right in the next town, only nine miles away.

It was the great Phineas Barnum and his show, fresh from Broadway. People said there was a woman in it who sang up higher than an angel, and a man and his wife no more than up to a man's coat pockets. Clowns of course. Three elephants. A zebra ringed like a broomstick.

My father yearned so to go to that circus he ached all over, and he could not get his Saturday morning hulled-corn down, though it was covered with molasses. He would never have dared to mention to his father his thought of going to see such a wonder, so expensive, so far away.

"William, you have been a good boy all the Spring and lugged in your wood without being told. Here's a silver dollar for you to spend. You take the steam-cars and go to the circus. And have a good time."

William found a shiny brand-new dollar in his hot hands almost as big as he was. He had never had so much wealth in his hands before. He forgot even to say "Thank you, sir." He grabbed his hat and coat and bolted for Cousin Trustum's house. William never thought of having a good time without having Trustum along.

To see zebras and Tom Thumb and hear Jenny Lind sing was the Promised Land of Canaan. But to ride to them all on the steam-cars of the brand-new *Portland and Kennebec Railroad* was heaven itself. The dust of that sleepy village street turned to a baby cyclone as a little boy flew along on his bare toes.

Trustum caught fire from my father. He ran shouting to his father that William had a whole silver dollar to spend and wanted to take him to see Barnum's. Trustum was a good head shorter than William, but William would take care of him. Could he go and could he have a dollar? Trustum's father could not be outdone by his brother. He fetched up a silver cartwheel from his jeans and gave it to his son.

So the two small boys ran hand in hand to the depot and the wonderful iron horse that snorted out steam and sparks.

But my father stopped short just at the depot and dug his toes into the Summer dust.

"Trustum, you and me are going to walk to Brunswick and save our dollar to spend all on Barnum's!"

It was the dawn of genius.

It was right then and there my father started being a man of wealth.

Trustum had tears in his blue eyes when he thought about the steam-cars. But he said nothing and plodded off down the road beside his longer-legged friend. William knew best. He always was right.

It was a long and hot nine miles, but they did it. They did

it fast. They let no dust settle on their long boy trousers; they
kept ahead of it. And they came up to a tame meadow with
tame white daisies in it, and there was a vast white tent that
looked for all the world like the City of Jericho Aunt Margaret read so much about in the *Bible*. And that canvas city
shook with music and the bellowings of elephants.

The two little boys came up to the wonder. But genius
struck my father again. He stopped Trustum dead in his
tracks just at the gate of the Promised Land.

"Trustum, you and me are going to work our way into this
circus and save our dollar to spend when we get in."

This time a tear leaked out of Trustum, but he swallowed
the rest. He was hot and tired as a dog, and his trousers were
dark where they touched him. But William must be right.
He followed my father round to the back way. There was a
man there filling up buckets of water for the elephants. He
was looking for two smart boys. William took Trustum's
coat and wide-visored new cap off for him, folded them on
his own. He rolled up Trustum's sleeves and his own, and
he sailed in. Trustum sailed in best he could behind him.
They tugged at pails half the size they were. They slopped
the buckets. They sopped their best trousers from *A* to *Z*, but
they watered down those elephants. One of the elephants got
playful and squirted water all over Trustum's ruffly blouse.
Trustum always caught it, not William. Trustum did not
mind, for after that, the elephant trumpeted. The zebra *was*
painted in rings like a broomstick, and he drank three buckets

of water. The boys even watered down some of the clowns. The clowns were painting themselves up for the afternoon, and they were dry as cork. One of them let Trustum put the red spots on him.

When two o'clock rolled round, the boys went in, sopped but brimming with joy, and sat down in the middle of the Promised Land in the very best seats. They tried out several. They left heart-shaped prints wherever they rested their trousers, but they dried off quick with the heat. And the two silver dollars were safe still in their rear pockets and left a print of Liberty right in their persons as they sat.

The band let out a snort and started in. A thousand people crowded into the benches. The elephants—the boys' elephants!—marched by big as continents. William was sure one recognized them and winked. He saw his eye-winkers move. The clowns *did* recognize them and waved to the boys. They cut up most of their capers near enough so William and Trustum could have put out their hands and touched them. They built themselves up a house, and it got afire, and the clowns slid down the roof on their billowing trousers and all of them missed the landing-net the firemen had spread out to catch them in. It was wonderful.

A lady all covered with shining stars walked out on a tight-rope so high up she looked like a butterfly. She carried a sunshade and a chair, and didn't she sit down in the chair right on nothing, and they brought out a whole tea-set and she took her tea right there in the air, cool as a cucumber! Tom

[15]

Thumb rode past behind ponies no bigger than dogs, in a coach no more than a baby-carriage. He had on striped trousers William could fill up, or even Trustum, but he was smoking a cheroot long as William's father's. He stood up and bowed this way and that to the applause.

But Jenny Lind was the best. She stood up on a platform, all white as an angel. She opened a little mouth, and songs came out of it and filled the vast tent full. Higher and higher she went till the flute could not follow her any more, and she was all alone. It was a miracle those notes from a small white throat could fill up a whole city made of white cloth! It was more like heaven than even the *Portland and Kennebec* steam-cars could ever hope to be. William felt he was floating on high Summer clouds. He would remember this singing all his life. And small Trustum got tears in his eyes again and almost ran over. But, this time, William did not mind a bit.

Two little boys brimful of elephants and music staggered down to the depot.

William put out his hand and stopped Trustum just when he had his foot up on the steps of the steam-car.

"You and me, Trustum," he said, "are going to walk home and save our dollar whole!"

So genius spoke once more. Trustum felt like crying, he was so tired. He did cry. But after he had done it and had got up off the railroad tie he had cried on, William dusted off his seat, and they started the long road home.

The shadows lengthened out across the world. The evening thrushes began to sing. Two slim boys wobbled on. Suddenly a very weary small boy sat smack down in the middle of the road in his velveteen trousers. He could no longer put one foot ahead of the other. He was done.

"Leg up, Trustum," said William. "Don't cry. I'll carry you pig-back the rest of the way."

And my father did. All those last three weary miles. The thrushes gave up singing, called it a day, and went to bed. The night-hawks began to zoom. My father's trousers bowed out heart-shaped with Trustum's weight. He stubbed both big-toes on stones in the dark. The stars came out. My father stopped oftener and oftener to rest, leaning his load, who had gone peacefully to sleep, against every tree he came to. But he never set his burden down. He never could have got it up again.

My father made it. And he delivered Trustum, and Trustum's silver coin, still unbroken, still unspent, into Trustum's father's arms.

And didn't Trustum's father, next day, borrow Trustum's dollar back for something and never return it!

But father's father never got William's back.

My father had his silver cartwheel safe. He put it away in his horsehide chest with the brass tacks that spelled out WILLIAM on the top.

That dollar became the nest-egg of my father's life-earnings. He had not eaten his cake, and he had it. And Barnum's glories, too. He never spent that old first dollar of his. He got to calling it his Jenny Lind Dollar. He looked at it every so often. Whenever he was tempted to lay out a lot of money on something, he remembered how he had earned his way to hear the Swedish nightingale sing and had saved his dollar. So he earned his way this once more.

The dollar was like a magnet. It attracted other dollars to it in that chest. Years went by. And so my father, on the edge of the grave, was able to give each of his ten children a house to live in.

And if you should open my father's grave, I think you would find that dollar, too dear to part with for Barnum and Tom Thumb and Jenny Lind, still with him yet. Unbroken, unspent, bright as that lovely nightingale's song a century ago, bright as I remember his smile.

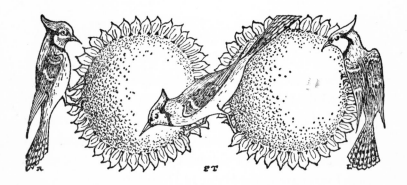

2. The Haunted Lobster-Warp

WE HAD just clattered in our hayrack across Dyke Bridge, and the horse was beginning to climb the hill past the Haunted House. It was a dark lowering day with low clouds, and it was now getting on towards sunset time, though there wasn't any sun to see. I did not feel very good. I never did when I was passing the Haunted House.

The house was haunted all right. My brother Ansel knew

[19]

it. I knew it. We had heard people talking. Little pitchers
have big ears. I was only seven, but I had very big ones.
Ansel was eight and going on nine, and he heard lots more
than I ever did. Yes, we had heard them—Ben Sudbury, the
hired-man, Uncle Thomas, and our father—when they didn't
think we were paying much attention. They talked the house
over. Saul Marriner had walled his wife right up in that
house's cellar alive.

We had often tiptoed in through the sagging front door
and peeked down there where the cellar stairs had been. We
had seen that wall. There it was, sealing off half a good cellar. And there were some three-toed tracks deep in the granite
ledge back of the bedroom Saul Marriner had died in. We
had seen them. Like a giant crow's tracks. They all pointed
straight towards Saul Marriner's room.

I don't think Ansel felt very good, either. But I never could
tell about Ansel. He never showed his feelings in his face.
He was just like an Indian: you never could tell by his face
how he felt.

It was lonesome and quiet. The empty hayrack rattled
and sounded awful loud. There wasn't a sign of wind under
all the heavy clouds. The old house with the blank windows
and gaping door was looming right over us. The horse was
picking up his feet and hurrying faster now. He always hur-
ried going past that house. He was anxious to get past it fast.
You can't fool a horse, Uncle Thomas always said. A horse
always knows. It was getting darker and lonesomer.

"Peter!"

Ansel reined old Dick in so sudden, I went forward smack into his seat, and he and I went smack into the front rail of the hayrack. We leaned like just one thin boy over the rail.

"Peter! Up there in the west bedroom." My brother's whisper was the only sound there was in the world, now the hayrack and the horse had stopped dead. "That rope on that old roped-bed! Enough rope for three good lobster-warps!"

We were at a crucial point in our lobstering. We had thirty traps we had made. Or rather Ansel had made. I had just held the bows for Ansel as he nailed on the laths. And we had only about twenty traps off and fishing because we had run out of rope. We had borrowed rope from our father here and there. But father had begun to miss his boat-painters and well-ropes, and he had threatened to tan our breeches for us if we helped ourselves to any more of his rope. We were desperate.

"Peter, you scoot right on up there and get that rope off the bed. Here's my knife, but don't cut it unless you have to. You work the knots loose with the blade. I'll hold the horse here and wait for you. Scoot now. And look alive. There's a smart boy."

"No." I whispered lower than my brother. "No," I said, "it's getting late. We've got to get on home. We'll get that rope another time. We'll come back for it tomorrow."

"We've got to have that rope tonight. You get up there

and work it off that bed." My brother's face was made up hard. There was no shaking him loose when his face was made up hard that way.

"You let me hold the horse, Ansel, and you go get the rope. You can get the knots out quicker'n I can. You know you can."

My brother's eyes blazed sparks under the low clouds.

"You little coward! What you scared of?"

"Nothing. But I ain't going one step."

"All right, you little yellow-belly. We'll both of us go!"

Ansel jumped down from the rack, twisted the horse's reins together fiercely, and made the horse fast to a young popple tree by the road's side.

"You march your boots along with me, yellow-belly!"

I went, but I went a good long ways behind Ansel. We came up to the tumbling doorstones and the sagging door. My brother went in and up the staircase. He creaked loud all the way. I went up after him, creaking quieter.

It was almost dark on the stairs. Our footfalls had started up all sorts of sounds in the crazy old house. They were going all around and up and down. I followed Ansel into the chamber. It was where Saul Marriner had died. It was a little lighter in the room there. There the bed was, just as Ansel had remembered it. It was crisscrossed with thick old manila, goodness knew how old. Fathoms and fathoms of wonderful lobster-warp. My brother whipped out his jack-knife and went at the knots.

We had to work fast, for what light there was left in the room was ebbing fast. I found a rusty old square nail, a homemade one, and set to on my side of the bed. Ansel got out three knots to my one. It was blistering hard work. But Ansel had a way with knots. We got the rope started. We got coils and coils of it loose on the floor. I never worked so fast in my life before. Ansel never did, either. It was getting darker and darker. It was also getting quieter and quieter. You could have heard a pin drop in the Doughty House two miles away, if there had been anybody there to drop a pin. There hadn't been for twenty years.

We had got down to the last row of knots, on the foot-rail of the bed. We had the rope nearly all loose.

"Hark!" I stood up from the knot I was in. I thought I heard something.

Mother of Moses! didn't that old Dick of ours tethered out there to the popple let out a squeal just then you could have heard in town. That horse whinnied up and up till my hair rose right up on end. Then there was a great clatter of our hayrack going away from there fast.

Ansel and I plunged to the window. We got there just in time to see Dick going. He had pulled that popple up by its roots. It was right out straight in the air behind his mane, and Dick was right out straight in the air ahead of it and sailing off over the hill, cart and all.

Golly! Ansel and I took out of that room, down those rickety stairs, over the doorsteps in one leap, and took off after our horse. We chased him nearly to the Doughty Place before he got tuckered out and slowed down so we could get our hands on the cart-tail. When we got up to him and retrieved the reins, he turned his head towards us. We could see his weather eye blazing like a big ball of red fire against the glooming west. The horse was all of a white lather, too, from head to tail, and trembling like a popple tree. That horse of ours was in an awful shape!

My brother Ansel tied up the broken reins, climbed right up into the cart, swung that horse and haycart around, and started back towards the Haunted House.

Once that brother of mine had his mind made up and his chin out, there was no arguing with him. I caught hold of the cart-rungs and held on. We flew back.

Dick tried his darnedest to lean away from that dark house as we hurtled back up to it, but Ansel yanked on the port rein and brought him smack up to the front door. There was a dead oak tree there. Ansel got out the halter and anchored the horse so he couldn't get loose unless he pulled that oak tree up by its roots.

"See here, Peter. You take this knife of mine. You go up there and cut those last knots right off. Get the rope and bring it down here to me."

But I had my chin set hard, too.

"I won't go. I won't go if you kill me!"

"Little yellow coward!" My brother hissed like an adder.

[24]

"Little girl in pants!" And my brother marched right into the dark house.

I marched in behind him and up the dead-dark stairs.

And just as we two came into that almost pitch-dark chamber-room, where something on three-toed feet like a bird had come to fetch Saul Marriner, the sun came suddenly out from under the clouds. It was sitting right on the edge of the world. Just as it went down, it lighted up that room through the western window clear as day.

There our rope was, and there the bed was. And wasn't that rope, every last fathom of it, back on the old bedstead— every last inch of it all tied right back into all its knots where it had been for all those years it had been up in that bedroom, where it had been the night the three-toed one came for Saul Marriner! Every knot tied tight again, every inch of the rope drawn taut again, all the rope back on that bed!

Two very small boys, with blond hair standing, came out of that house like bright bullets, cut off their halter, lashed up the horse, and went bouncing off down the road home, with the horse leveling out in the air, and their wheels touched earth only now and then on a few high places here and there.

3. Teddy Roosevelt

I GUESS you couldn't think up a more typical American design than this: Two small tousled and freckled American boys in overalls and bare feet, fishing, and right between them an amber-eyed American bald-headed eagle superintending their fishing, with lightning in his eyes.

But you don't need to think that design up. It actually happened once. I was one of the two boys that sat beside the eagle. It was our eagle, too, our pet eagle on Paradise Farm.

He had a good American name, he was a good American bird, and he had a fine American burial on the Fourth of July.

I, Peter, was responsible for him, really. For I found him. First, anyway. All my many brothers, and a whole parcel of he-cousins, said they would have found him if I hadn't. He was so big a bird, right there in the middle of the pasture, that nobody could ever have missed him. That's what they all said, to take the wind out of my sails.

Father was responsible for his name, though he never was consulted about it. Father had sulked for some years because he hadn't been allowed to name his youngest son Theodore Roosevelt. Father liked to name sons after Presidents—current Republican ones, that is. I have a brother Benjamin Harrison. When I came along, father was sulking like Achilles in his tent during Cleveland's second administration, so there was no chance then. But brother Frank hove along right when Teddy Roosevelt was flowering towards the Presidency. My father knew he would become President even before McKinley got shot.

Theodore Roosevelt was a man after my father's own heart. He had a big family, he was a fighter, he liked he-ness and the strenuous life in the outdoors. He even looked like my father. So father had set his heart on having a son with his name. But mother had put her foot down. Theodore Roosevelt was much too much of a mouthful to say. And, anyway, mother did not want to have a whole houseful of Presidents. She had to stop father somewhere. So she stopped him at Theodore Roosevelt.

We decided on the name for our eagle in solemn conclave in the woodshed. We jumped at the chance to make it up to our father for his bitter disappointment. And our eagle, by the time we named him, had become an exponent of the strenuous life again, as much as a bird with only one wing could. So we named our eagle Theodore Roosevelt.

I was going after the cows when I stumbled upon Theodore Roosevelt. It was dim going. A fog had come in over Misery Hill, and Seguin foghorn was lowing like a vast lonesome cow. I could not see more than ten feet before me. But I knew where the cows would be of a foggy night, and I was making a bee-line for the Upper Beeches.

Going after the cows was my province. I did most of my best thinking then. I did not have to pay any attention to my feet. They knew the way and twinkled along white and independent. I could give my whole time to my thinking.

I was doing that this night, but I became aware that a woman was there by me. She was sitting not five feet away from the cow-path I was going on. I half-noticed that she was an old woman, hunched up, and she had a white shawl over her shoulders. Suddenly, when I had got past her, I stopped. It struck me that an old woman ought not to be sitting out there in a fog on a stump in our pasture that way. I turned around and went back to look her over. When I got up to her, she turned her head, and I saw she had a hooked nose too sharp and long for even a very old woman, and her port eye blazed out at me with a flash of lightning. She was no woman at all. She was a huge bald eagle.

The eagle's wing was clamped tight in a large trap. The trap was chained to a log. The log was there. The bird had uprooted it and dragged it along with him, goodness knows how far. It was no trap of ours. It looked big enough for a man.

I streaked it home with my feet going high as my head behind me. I forgot all about the cows. I told my brother and a big cousin. They came running back with me, but they could barely keep my two footsoles in sight.

The older boys took off their coats. It was Saturday night, and they had their best coats on. They threw their coats over the eagle's head, and the eagle slashed them into ribbons with his talons. They kept throwing the shreds of their coats back, though, and finally wound the eagle all up in wool. Then they took his wing out of the trap, carried him home to the woodshed on a pole, and got out their scalpels. My brother Edward had aspirations to become a surgeon. The wing was all festered up to the second joint. They gave the bird a whiff of ether, they amputated most of the wing, bandaged up the stump, pouring on carbolic acid, and carried the sorry-looking eagle to my playhouse and threw him in.

Mine was only a small, mean playhouse. But it was all I had. It was all my brothers would build me. It never occurred to the boys to pick on any of my brothers' or sisters' houses. They picked on mine. The eagle, when he came to, screamed all night and made a shambles of my clay statuary there. He messed up my carpet.

The operation was a complete success.

For weeks the boys fed the eagle through my window, in the ruins of my sculptures. They fed him fish, clams and crabs, and meat, in great quantities. They finally let the bird out and gave him the run of the yard. He tried once or twice to get aloft, on his one good wing and the stump, but each time he tried it he came back on his back, stunned. He gave in to his fate, then, and walked the yard, shouldering ahead side to side with his high shoulders. He was taller than I was standing up. He was the biggest eagle I ever heard tell of. He flourished, his wing healed up. He grew accustomed to us and stopped trying to slice off our hands when we tossed food to him. We christened him then—Theodore Roosevelt.

Theodore learned the ropes. He learned fast. He learned that hens and ducks and geese were part of the family and were not to be eaten. It took him five or six weeks, and five or six hens or ducks or so, and an imprisonment in my ruined house after each mistake, before he learned. My mother was patience itself, though she was often bitter.

Teddy also finally learned that my yellow dog Snoozer was not legal tender, either. But only after Snoozer had lost a small bit off his tail and been marked for life on his flank with furrows made by Teddy's claws. And Snoozer, to the end of Teddy's stay with us, respected the bird and gave him a very wide berth.

Theodore learned at length to let us do his hunting for him. We had to do plenty. That bird ate twice his weight, I vow, in meat or fish every day. It kept us hustling, providing. Especially me. I would bring up a half peck of clams, crack them for the eagle, and he would swallow them, and some of their shells with them, and keep up with me fast as I could go. He would blink his eyes for more. He got so he knew my fingers from the fish in my fingers and took the fish without paring off my nervous digits. I have several scars, though, from the days when Teddy was learning.

As the Summer went by, Theodore Roosevelt grew from mere respect for us children to a kind of affection. As much affection as the king of all birds could decently show. We would be playing somewhere, and a shadow would come, we would look up, and there the great dark bird was in his wide white collar, in the very midst of us as we tumbled and played. He looked on, quiet, and in vast dignity. Wherever we were, he would suddenly be gravely there. He would turn his beak side to side, tip one eye our way, and watch our antics with tolerance and interest. He became one of us. He even tolerated Snoozer, though his deep-set eyes would kindle whenever he looked Snoozer's way. He thought about all that meat, alive and tender. But he resisted temptation, for he knew Snoozer was ours.

Our eagle would come up to us of his own accord, even

when it was not feeding time, and he would let us scratch him on one spot on the back of his magnificent, broad, snake-like head. He liked that. He would close his eyes, his pink lids rising up from the bottom of his eyes, and think gentle thoughts. We could see Theodore think them.

Theodore was a noble sight among all our tabby friends in the yard, among the geese and the ducks. He was a little humorous, too. For we never could get over the impression when he walked that he was like a man losing his trousers. His pants seemed forever down around his feet.

Oh, Theodore made some mistakes, even to the end. But they were almost always forgivable ones. Once he ruined a circus of ours. We had been sweating all day long digging out a woodchuck to act as our brown bear in the animal tent. Snoozer had buried himself to his tail in the woodchuck's burrow and been bitten badly. But we had our bear. He was to be the star of our afternoon performance. We had tethered him in a collar and chain in the yard and gone in to our dinner.

We had forgotten all about Theodore Roosevelt. We were eating our tapioca pudding when disaster fell. We heard that high-pitched scream that meant Teddy was on the warpath, the scream he gave in moments of exhilaration and joy. We ran out. But we were too late. There sat Theodore in the ruins of our brown bear. He had taken the woodchuck apart in two slashes of his wicked claws. The woodchuck was all over the yard. He was a total loss. Theodore had as much of a smile on his face as his wicked scimitar of a beak would permit. He had swallowed some tasty portions of our newest pet already. He looked up with pride for our approval. Teddy knew that woodchuck was wild. You couldn't fool him on a woodchuck. He knew he was not like the geese and the ducks. So he had sailed into him. It was the first hunting he had had in months. He was proud as a peacock. We couldn't find it in our hearts to scold him.

The bird we had taken into the family never came quite in. He kept some reservations of the wild. There was always that wild cry of his, at his eating, at his peaks of joy. It always sent a thrill and a chill down our spines. Theodore could not suppress it when he swallowed an especially large mussel or half of a crab. And Teddy never ate anything gently. He wolfed everything. He used his talons like knives. He was wonderful strong. He would put one claw on a flounder, lean over and take the flounder's head in his beak, and tear the whole fish in two, backbone and all, in one lightning movement.

Theodore Roosevelt would have moments when all gentleness would wash out of his golden eyes, he would look up at the sky and become, in an instant, a wild and untouchable thing. Especially when birds sailed over, the eagle would have those moments of sudden transformation. And for whole days, sometimes, when the mood was on him, he would go off by himself, shouldering his way out of our lives, past the ducks and hens, through the firs and junipers, up into the pasture, and there he would sit on some headland and gaze straight into the sun or off where the high Atlantic met the sky. He would sit there for hours with the sunlight blazing on the snow of his neck and on his bronze shoulders, alone, lonesome. He would stare into the sun and into the blue vastness of sea and sky where he belonged, that he had been a high part of once, when he had been whole and free. It made us all kind of sad.

Of course, on those days of his return to eagledom, Theodore fasted. And of course it was some relief not to have to rustle quahaugs and crabs for him! It was a pleasant vacation. Especially for me. For my older brothers had by this time turned over to me most of the management of Teddy's commissariat.

Yet, most of the time, Theodore, for all his natural loneliness and epic size and appearance, fitted surprisingly well into our large and boisterous family. Even father—never very grateful, we discovered, for our attempt to heal his broken heart by perpetuating his favorite President's name on our bird—came to look on Teddy as one more of his boys. He saved up choice tidbits of cods' tongues and sounds for him and fed them to the bird himself. Teddy would sit with his head back beaming and waiting for the bliss.

Our bird early discovered the source of most of his food. He learned at once to associate fish-poles with feasting. The minute we boys came out of the house with our poles, he came shouldering his way across the yard hot-foot, and fell right in behind us. He followed us down to the source of supply. He took his place on the bank right beside us, with expectation in his eyes. I swear he learned to know when we had a bite. He would cock his head and become restless. We might grow drowsy with the Summer and our heads nod. But not Teddy's. He noticed the bobbing of our poles. He became taut. He made a hissing sound in his beak. I swear he even nudged us with a shoulder and warned us to pull in.

When we reeled in a fish, Teddy became electrified. He leaped three feet into the air, let out his hunting warwhoop, caught the fish in one claw, at the hook's end, and with his beak he tore off half the eel or flounder and swallowed it before he struck the ground. He had learned to swallow the lower end and not the hook-end of the fish. For we had had to give him ether twice to get a hook out of him when he had swallowed the bow-end of the fish. He never made that mistake, or any other, three times.

Often, when the brother nearest to me and I were fishing, Theodore Roosevelt would sit right in between us on the ledge. His finely carved head topped our two yellow ones. People going by on the sea were taken by surprise, seeing the three of us there together. They squealed in terror and admiration. I suppose it was a shock of the first water to strangers to see two small barefooted boys with fish-poles sitting with a great white-collared emblem of our American democracy between them, all three intent on catching flounders! It was something out of a story-book.

Summer turned to Winter, and Teddy had to follow us out on the bay ice to get his eels and smelts fresh. He holed up in my playhouse and completed the ruin of it in the time of deep snows. When Spring came, he was one of the first of us on the clam flats. He walked behind us boys dredging up the broken clams as his own. He even got so he would ride in the boat with us, on the stern seat. That was a sight to make a strange lobsterman's eyes bug. An eagle sitting in a boat's stern and cutting flounders in two in the air as we brought them in!

But when the leaves came on the trees again, at about the time I had found him the year before, Teddy sickened and slowed down. He went on no more fishing trips with us. Something had gone wrong with his wing. My surgeon brother was called in. He took off more of the bone. For a time, the eagle brightened. But he sickened again. His great amber eyes came open less and less when we came to visit him in his corner of the yard. My brother made a last desperate operation. But no go. Next morning the eagle lay like a ruined mountain on the grass. He had the good American instinct to die on the day before the Fourth of July.

We buried Theodore Roosevelt with full military honors, and a salute from all our different-calibered guns and rifles, in the dolls' graveyard beyond the Upper Pasture bars, in the blazing sun of the Fourth. Wild roses had just come out on the ledges, and the girls made a garland of those. And I went to my father's G.A.R. stores and got out one of his largest cotton flags. I set it in the earth over Theodore's grave.

So the Stars and Stripes flew over the grave of the totem of our Republic. It was fine to know that flag was there over the head of a child of the sun and sky who had come to live a year in our family and go fishing with young American boys, who had worn on his proud, high shoulders the name of one of the best of our Presidents.

4. The Harvest of Diamonds

Today is a "diamond-dust day," as Maine people describe it, such a day as only middle Winter brings. There is terrific sunshine. There is terrific wind. Every snowdrift smokes at its edge with powdered diamonds that blind the eyes.

Such a day, when I was a boy many years ago, would have seen one of Maine's best harvests in full swing. It was a harvest that brought millions of dollars into thousands of homes.

It was a harvest that took nothing out of the soil, nothing out of the state. Yet it was a heavy crop and weighted down a thousand schooners sailing the two greatest oceans, rounding Cape Horn and Good Hope.

It was ice. The harvest that electricity has almost erased from the world.

On such a Winter day as this, years ago, every road and railroad track leading to the Kennebec River would have been black with men, walking. They walked down from the upper part of the state, in from New Hampshire, up from Massachusetts. They walked railroad tracks because the railroads would not let them ride. For every man-jack of them was shod with steel, and the calks on his shoes would have cut the train floors to pieces. Those shoes were life to the wearers; the men never stepped out of them all the weeks they worked. Those shoes cut the railroad ties to sawdust. The ends of all the sleepers, outside the rails, were worn down to the gravel when the ice season was over. Men's feet had worn the railroad out!

All Maine farmers, with their fields under snow and nothing to be gathered there, became, for five or six weeks, gatherers of squared diamonds cut out of the sparkling Kennebec and shipped across the continent and to the corners of the world to keep food and people cool in Summer.

The ice companies had to build huge sheds to house these harvesters at night, and furnish each man with a blanket. One man was told off to keep the single stove going. The other men lay down in windrows in their calked boots. They were packed in like sardines on the floor, and they had to turn over on the other side all at the same time. "Break joints!" was the cry, and the men rolled over in unison. The workers slept with their picks, too. They had brought them from home; they knew their potentialities and powers by heart. They had to, for their lives depended on the steel points they had sharpened. A dull point might mean a cold grave thirty feet deep. An ice cake handled wrong could break a man's back.

After a gigantic breakfast of meal gruel in the eating places of Gardiner, Richmond, or Bowdoinham, the men went out on the fields on the river that had been staked off with brush. There scrapers were dragging off the night's snow and frost or windscuff. Behind them came the ice markers, plows drawn by one horse, which lined off the field into a checker-board of twenty-two-inch squares. Back of these the two-horse groovers came, one after the other, with teeth gradu-ated at a slant to cut a progressive cut, five inches, seven inches, ten, twelve inches deep. These plows of the water were all made by the same firm: first *Gifford and Wood,* later *Wood and Sons.*

It was a great sight for a boy to see, the fine horses coming with plumes at each nostril, the plows ripping through the ice behind with sparks of ice flying, the brawny men holding the groovers' handles with their gates-ajar moustaches fringed with frosty breath. Not many such sights in the world this side of Homer!

So the fields were made ready, and the cakes took final form, standard the world over, twenty-two by forty-four inches, for the groovers took only every other mark in the cross-hatching the markers had made when they grooved the field lengthwise. The cakes were ready now to be broken apart, each still dry and joined to all the others by the three inches of ice left exquisitely unflawed at the bottom of the field and still capable of holding up all the ice-kings' horses and all the ice-kings' men. The river from Augusta to Bath was dotted with smoking horses and smoking men.

Now two husky sawyers cut a canal, only a bit wider than the lengths of the rectangles of ice, from the field to the ice-house on the bank where a steam engine worked an endless chain with oak lugs a dozen feet apart. The last diamond-cutting began. The breakers of diamonds, armed like Neptune with their three-pronged "busting-bar," started taking the field apart. The calkers went ahead of them and closed up the seams of the cakes remaining as each row of cakes was broken free. For if the water got into the cuts, they would heal up, and all the grooving would have to be done over. The breakers walked along, striking here and there with their bars, the ice sighed, and long rows of diamonds broke off, submerged, and rose to the top of the water. Men with picks nosed these lines of squared jewels up the canal

[41]

and floated them on to the house. At the foot of the run, two giants took turns "busting" the cakes apart. The engine chugged, the lugs caught the cakes, the cakes shot shining up in a long slant on the sky to the high door of the ice-house.

Some of these icehouses were larger than the chateaux of France. Six hundred feet long, some of them. With double pine walls upholstered with sawdust between. The runs could be extended upward as the houses filled towards their eaves. As each cake of ice plunged up into the house, it shot through a planer, gauged to cut all cakes to that particular day's thickness, so the tiers would be uniformly thick. The cakes leapt out of the planer upon the fan-tail, full of great momentum still. Here was the hot spot most boys loved to stand at. Here was the most motion, most speed and danger. The blue diamonds came in like things wicked and alive, they struck the oak fan-tail, and the switchers caught them delicately on their picks, shunted them this way and that, with the speed of light, and let them roar on along the proper tracks that led to the tiers. The diamonds ran on their own power still till they reached the exact spot where the stowers wanted them to lie. They had to be humored in handling, for, in spite of their heft, they were fragile as glass and easily broken. The vast cathedral of ice was full of thunder as the ice cakes came running, full of the thunder of men's shouts as they coaxed the cakes into place.

The tiers rose fast. A space of two inches was left between

the cakes. But when men and cakes touched the roof, a top layer, the "plugger," was put on crosswise with its cakes touching, to bind all together against warm weather. Marsh hay was heaped over the top. The house was sealed, full to the eaves. The army of men moved on, engine and all, to the next cathedral of Winter.

So the crop was garnered in. And Kennebec preachers thanked God for sending Maine zero weather, and some of them, I know for a fact, thanked God for keeping the rival Hudson unfrozen. Thaws and warm spells might come, but there was the Kennebec adage that "Winter has never rotted in the sky yet," and that other one, "Never too late to cut ice till the robins sing." And the farmers went back with fat wallets to their farms rejoicing and wearing the railroad ties down to the bone.

But when the ice broke up in the Spring, in those days of rich harvests, there would always be ten or so bodies of stout men picked up at the Kennebec's mouth, men with the calked boots still on their feet. The river took its harvest, too.

Spring brought the schooners. Vessels from Singapore, Yokahama, Batavia, San Francisco, and Calcutta lay side by side at Iceboro and Swan Island in my river. The ice slid into their holds and was stanchioned firm and braced against the roll of the sea. And the schooners went off over the whole globe, and yellow men and black men and brown men who lived in perpetual Summer put sparkling Maine and Winter into their mouths, and wonder lit their eyes.

[43]

Today the great cathedrals are gone. Gone away into the smoke that took many of the icehouses till insurance companies refused to insure them, gone rotting into the ground beside caves still intact where the Abenaki Indians refrigerated their sturgeon and deer three hundred years ago. But now and then you can come upon tools made by *Wood and Sons* in Kennebec haymows, and you may fall in with an old man who stood up on calked shoes with his spear in Maine's epic age, when Maine diamonds kept the whole world fresh and cool.

5. The Picnic Problem

Most people watch the approach of the picnic season with equanimity, and even joy. But not I. I have too many scars of bygone picnics upon me. I watch the open season come as I would the foliation and flowering of poison ivy. Picnics are, unless properly handled by experts such as myself, just about as poisonous. It is not without significance that most picnics do finish up in a vigorous patch of poison ivy in full bloom. Disasters attract disasters. The immortal stars attend to such concatenations of woe.

I believe that the chief trouble with picnics is that they are too well planned and too weighted down with improper paraphernalia. And too often the wrong people superintend them. Indoors people. People who require all the refinements of the modern kitchen to cook the smallest hamburger. Dishes, of any kind, are perfect conductors to misfortune. And, of course, children are an invitation to tragedy. They should not be, for children are the real centers to picnics. But the way picnics are usually run, they are encouraged to be practically lightning-rods to attract the worst meteorology and Providence can offer. Uncles and aunts are also disastrous. But I imagine it is rather late in history to eliminate *them* from picnic problems.

Really, the safest picnic is one a man takes, *solus,* with a fishing-rod, a hunk of salt pork and a frying pan, and a quart of Scotch. Women, children, dogs, salt, pepper, thermos-jugs, and green salads are invitations to complicated trouble.

But leaving all his people out, I suppose, is the coward's way in picnics. Most men have women and children and friends and thermos-bottles and picnic baskets in their homes they cannot bypass. Troubles are endemic with picnics. There is no charitable way around them. So you must go through.

Yet even in such complications as I mention, if you can keep your strategy simple, your dishes and cooking utensils down to the severest minimum, then, in spite of friends, in spite of creatures in skirts, or in trousers which are contoured in all the wrong places, in spite of boys, contoured correctly in the proper places, but so short in their pants that poison ivy has a practically unlimited field of operation, you can still bring off a normal picnic without physical or spiritual casualties—at least without mortal ones.

I have a lot of inventions up my sleeve which will revolutionize and humanize picnics and render them practically fool-proof.

First on the agenda is my non-upsettable bottle. Some of the deepest woes at picnics have come out of the fact that the drinking water has been spilled right at the start, and so everybody has gone about all the livelong day with a tongue swollen with thirst. Of course, the most flavorful food has been as ashes on such a tongue. So I am going to sponsor a bottle that, the instant it is turned on its side by the inevitable puppy or aunt whose five fingers are all thumbs, will—by centrifugal or some such force—arm itself with an inner stopper that will instantly close the nose up. It will be self-sealing. How that inner seal will be unstoppered later, I don't know exactly. But ways will be found, by me or by some other genius. We have self-sealing gas-tanks which can heal themselves up from bullet holes in our airplanes. Why shouldn't we have jugs which can heal themselves up from boys, puppy-and-aunt-proof ones, for our innocent lemonades and coffee? Let the experts in times of war put their brains to work on my brilliant idea for peace and figure the details out. They can. After all, I cannot do all the work. I furnish the ideas.

Deep into my brain is burned the memory of the time when I, my whole quiverful of offspring, and all my best friends went one whole day, on an island in the bitter sea, and off, on beach and on boat, without a drop to drink. A willful island goat upset our thermos of spring water right at the start. He was a he-goat and full of masculine imagination. He knew where to hit us just where it hurt most. First, he started tearing one of our company's picnic pants apart with his young horns when the owner of them was far off on the sea, swimming towards Spain. When the man's wife retrieved the pants, he stood up to her menacing her with his horns. I intervened. The pants and wife were saved. But the goat was angry at me. He bided his time. When I was bedding our clams down in hot rockweed among glowing coals, he came over against me sudden, head down, hell for leather, and sparks in his eyes. He caught me in my base sector like a bolt from the blue, and sent me up to my neck— the wrong way in—in the embers. Then while I was combing the coals from my curls, the goat ran against our thermos-jug and upset our whole waterworks. When in wrath I anchored him offshore in our tender, as a punishment, he chewed off the cord on our oarlocks and lost them on the bottom of the ocean. The rest of the day, after our lobsters and clams had filled us with their savory salts, we suffered with the blue damned through all the blue and blazing hours with a raging passion for liquid. We felt like the Ancient Mariner. We finally saved our dwindling reasons by each seizing a can of condensed milk, tapping it, and letting it dribble down our parched throats. If our thermos had had my self-sealing inner cap, that goat would not have ruined our day.

A non-puncturable paper bag is next on the docket. Never have I seen a bag of any sort that did not let the salt and pepper out or the red and black ants in. With the age of dresses of glass and flexible chromium pants right upon us, it is a disgrace we do not have a bag that ten small, squirming boys and a dog can sit on for four hours in a beach-wagon, yet will still pour out undefiled, sandless salt, sugar, or coffee. I have drunk so many ants in my coffee's sugar at picnics, I am certainly one part formic acid, and I am getting good and tired of such lack of imagination and progress. I must put my brain at work upon my bag.

Then, I will put my mind on my all-purpose eating tool. It will eliminate the fork, the spoon, the knife, and the drinking straw. It will be all of them, in turn, at the flip of a lever. It will cut like a pair of shears into the toughest salami, and it will also spread out points to pierce the stoutest hotdog. And between the tines it will be webbed as is the amphibious mallard, and it will dip up a man-sized portion of hot fish chowder. It will cut like a razor, on one edge, and on the other like a crinkled bread knife. It will be a marvel. It will revolutionize our morals and manners. You will be able even to open cans with it, both circular and flat ones, in the twinkle of an eye. Maybe you will be able to fell growing trees with it!

For people invariably do fell green-growing maples at picnics, just to make the business of kindling the fire a desperate and impossible task. That is one of the insoluble problems of picnics. With whole forests of dry brush and dead windfall boughs to draw on, why on earth do people make a bee-line for the only leafy trees about and cut down wood full of water and sap that even no archangel, or better, no arch-fiend, could ignite? The introduction of the idea of using dry kindling and brush alone would christianize the pagan passions of picnics.

But my best bet is my picnic suit. Ponchos were good, in their day. We always served them to our children, when they were growing up in spite of our frequent Summer picnics. I had brought home some ponchos from my war. They were absolutely *de rigueur* with my cods'-head chowder. We put the child's head through the hole, armed him with a spoon I made out of a clamshell stuck on a split stick, set him down in front of the chowder kettle, gave him a Boston cracker to heal the burns in his mouth, and let him hoe in.

But the time has come for a covering that will protect all the picnicker's body. Our offspring used to get their feet and fingers into the hot brew, in spite of the poncho's protection. What is needed is a light covering that will completely cover

Lowell's Cove, Orr's Island

a picnicker's every extremity. I have such a garment in mind. You will be able to sit in it in the midst of the most poisonous ground-oak and eat in perfect peace. Only the mouth will be exposed. I do not yet know what this picnic diving-suit will be made of. But it will be somewhat cellophanic, and it will be tough and unpuncturable as steel. You will be able to see through it perfectly, too. So all the comeliness of female or infant contours will still lend a central charm to the picnic and be the major spur to the male's desire to show off his prowess in creation of tasty roasts before admiring eyes of children and ladies. With one swoop, this transparent, flexible diving-bell of a play-suit will make all picnics free of all wounds save mouth burns and love bruises. The barbs of love enter through the eyes, and are sweet. So I suppose we shall still have to have them as major problems at our picnics. I, for one, want to retain them. And my diving-bell will increase their potency, I believe, by casting a glassy nimbus around them and stepping up their frequency.

Now that I have revolutionized the mechanics of the picnic, let me see what I can do for its social and economic angles. There is a vast area for improvement left, goodness knows. Let me trim the angles down smooth with a few *don'ts*.

First of all, don't go a long ways from home. It is a frequent mistake in picnics that people go far afield for the green and blue life they want to drink in. They go into unknown woods, fall into uncharted wells, tear their pants on foreign barbed wire, run into fields of no-trespassing, get shot at by lords of strange manors, and soak up unheard-of poisons among unplumbed poison growths. They set unfamiliar woods ablaze. Whereas if they stayed near home, they could ignite friends' forests, trespass on kindly people; they would know the fauna and flora and the sharp tongues among their neighbors, follow the contours of known disasters by swamp and hedge, take their mishaps with zest and not come to them worn down by travel. They could run home easily for unneeded extra cooking utensils they had forgotten and uncalled-for packets of first-aid. They would have more time for splendid lost motion which makes up most of the activities of picnics. They could be more interior than ever and set up whole suites of dining and living rooms on this known terrain. They could enjoy the usual mistakes with extra zeal.

Half the wear and tear of picnics could be avoided at the start if people would not combine a travel-tour with housekeeping outdoors and living off the ozone. The impedimenta for the long trip—and this includes all uncles—are deadly. For if you pack yourselves up with folding-chairs, you can just bank on it that you will inevitably try to use them, they will fold up on you in the soft earth and pinch you at your tenderest parts, and there's an end to serenity. Go into the woods next door, go up into the trees next lot, go down to your own beach and eat the sand with your sandwiches there, climb the local mountain. Fly not to the Andes and Lake Superiors you know not of!

Beach-wagons are bad enough. But boats are worse. Eschew them all. One of our largest and most elaborate family picnics—and we ran to large ones when our children were growing up—was ruined by a motor boat. We hired it. A big one, fit to transport a legion. We all piled on, including a dozen babes-in-arms and Phi Beta Kappa, the fox-terrier of our clan, with mountains of refreshments, even to watermelons and whole bunches of bananas. Then we pushed off for the day's revels and the family picnic-grounds, the island, far at sea, which my mother gave me in an unguarded moment when I wasn't looking. We were outfitted for at least a week's sojourn in the wilderness. We had the mothers equipped to feed the unweaned babies. We had everything. We piled all decks high.

And the boat caught afire.

It wasn't a bad fire. It was just a modest one. But it was pretty continuous. We would get it put out with sand and soda. But it would break out, like the measles, in another place. We smoked all the way down the bay. My mother was game. She had set her heart on going out to the family island, and she was not going to be turned back. I think the skipper set the fires on purpose, because the wind was kicking up a nasty chop, and he had cold feet about going so far from home. Anyway, the fires went on. And it got rougher and rougher. Phi Beta Kappa became deathly seasick and made a hideous mess of the quarter-deck. Babies rolled in the bilge. My mother set her jaw like granite and cried, with Columbus, "Sail on!"

But the lily-livered aunts hoisted the white flag. They prevailed on the craven captain. I think they were in cahoots. So we had to put in at a neck of the mainland and spread our picnic there. We could have walked to the place from home. And there we had come twenty-five miles by car and fifteen by boat, back almost to our own sea-dooryard! We had to eat up all that food for the wilderness at one sitting. We nearly foundered. It was a shambles of a picnic. The skipper put off in his craft and sailed home, unburning and chuckling. Nothing tasted right. The watermelons turned out all green. The children ate green apples, as children always do at picnics, and got doubled up with cramps. I think it finally came on a rain and wet us sopping.

By all means, finally, chloroform the ones among you who expect a four- or five-course banquet of a picnic, and leave them all at home. Your best picnic is a one-course affair. Roasting-ears, if that is what you yearn for, or plain steamed clams. But not both. Have one main dish and one only. Hotdogs or hamburg. Fringe your dish around with doughnuts and coffee, if you wish. But leave it the single rock of your regard. Be like the Indian. He knew his picnic. He lived on one all the days of his life. He never mixed meats. He was wise. Caribou or buffalo, or dog. But just that one dish.

And he lived fat and grew handsome. Stick to one dish. And shoot the aunt who brings cucumber sandwiches. Cucumbers never should go into sandwiches in any case. Outdoors, in bread, they are as poisonous as the copperhead. Sandwiches are the tenderfoot's idea of a picnic. I like them all right, on occasion. But the occasion should be the pick-up meal, and the sandwiches should be eaten at the kitchen table.

I recall the two best kinds of picnic I have ever been on. One is the kind I used to have with my father, when I was one of his host of worshipping small boys. He would take us out lobstering in his boat, and when we came in under the cold October stars, he would send us to cut dead-spruce brush and gather driftwood. He would sling his kettle, which he always toted in his dory, on a green fir-bole, and boil his lobsters under the high sky till the smell of them must have tempted the angels. Then he turned them out red in the light of our bonfire's embers, and we sailed in. We ate lobsters, sans bread, sans butter, sans everything but the hunger of a small boy, which is sharper than any Gallic sauce ever made. We ate lobster till it shone out at our smoky eyes. And father told us stories, shouting over the night wind, and we sucked lobster claws, being unable to get any more of the pink meat into our taut bodies. And we were very happy little boys, warmed with our ruddy coals and our lobsters in the vast blue-black wilderness of blazing stars.

My own best picnic is descended from my father's true pioneer model. When the urge to eat in the open falls upon me, as fall it must on all Americans with pioneers in their family trees, I take my dipnet and frying pan. A hunk of salt pork in my pants' pocket is all the indoors food I carry. I hie me hence to Spinney's Creek, under the frosty waning moon of April. I find me a place where the brook comes downstairs. Then I kindle a fire of fragrant spruce boughs, cut up my pork, put it in the pan. I take up my net and stand ready where the firelight shines on the water. Soon I see the slender and tender silver arrows come darting through the air up my stairs. I put my net under the smelts and flip them over into my frying pan where the salt pork is all sizzling ribbons. The fish hiss and brown up tender in the tender night. I dip them out one by one, as they come to a complete crisp, and swallow them down hot, eyes and fins and tails and entrails, in a brown brittle of delight. No bread, no doughnuts, no sandwiches. I take my whole feast out of the running water of the night. I take my whole meal out of the starry hand of Nature. And Nature is proud of me; up there among her stars, the old lady is proud of me as she was proud of her Indian children many, many moons ago.

Come, let us be Americans. Let us go Indian again when we go on our picnics this Summer!

6. The Thousand-Mile Duck

THE three men were loaded for bear all right, though they were bound for duck. The car was chockful of he-ware—Bud's twelve-gauge Parker that had gone through so many shooting seasons its barrel was paper-thin, Jim's leather-upholstered hunting pants so stout in the seat and crotch they could stand up all by their lonesomes, Bob's Lefever Nitro-Special, Jim's choke-bore British job of an eight-gauge, black-powder shells, smokeless shells, dubbing for shoes, high-lace boots, thermos-bottles, flashlights, waders, a pneumatic pillow which could also be used as a life-preserver, and—the soul and heart of all the gear and the gunning trip—five quarts of good Scotch.

The only she-thing in the loaded car was Mrs. Bob's handwritten receipt-book. Bob had borrowed it, unbeknownst to her, so he could run up a pan of the cream-o'-tartar biscuits, which were the center of his married life and which Bob could not get along without, from his wife's star receipt.

Behind the three men hot for holiday the November sky was crisscrossed with chevrons of mallards, redheads, canvasbacks, and teal, and Cayuga Lake was loud with hundreds of game birds. But the man from Maine transplanted to Upstate New York gripped the wheel and headed east. He was going to show his York-State friends some real he-man duck shooting on his own boyhood saltwater bays. He put his foot down hard on the gas. The car picked up speed and got the bone in her mouth. They were off on their five-hundred-mile journey, over farmlands, over a half dozen rivers, the Appalachians, over tidal marshes and fells, to the Atlantic.

The three gunners had enough shells to sink a gunning-float, tobacco enough for a week's steady smoking day and night, minds bristling full of brawny tales they had saved up for just such a he-picnic, and not a shaving brush, razor, or piece of soap among them. They had Scotch. Behind them were politeness and good manners, all women, for once, all their children, all little boys with big eyes and big questions, household chores, civic sense, wiping their feet on the porch mat, and jobs. Before them were four days of boyhood again, breathing in the smell of wild outdoors, and living off the country like the pioneers. They headed east into wild ducks and glory.

The men had left word with their wives that they wanted a bang-up hunt-supper on their return. They would bring home the makings. So the women were left greasing up the bake-pans and spits and sending out the invitations.

Along the Mohawk it began to come in spitting snow. They were in for a regular spell of hunting weather. It made them feel like boys. They burst into *Cristofo Colombo,* a song not meant for indoors. But the spitting snow turned into a no'theast blizzard by the time they were over the Berkshires. It plastered up the windshield till they had to manipulate the wipers by hand and ride with both doors open. Bob had to drive with one hand and with one good eye peering out at the side of the car into a world of blind white. Jim, snoozing with his homemade mittens on his lap, woke up with a start when they brought up on a bank and caromed back on the road, and threw one of his mittens out of Bud's door. They stopped and hunted for it, pawing in the snow, but had to give the family heirloom up for lost. Jim had to put both hands into his one mitten the rest of the outing.

They came to the coast at dark and bucked into a howling gale off the Atlantic. But the snow let up. Their teeth rat-

tled. The York men spelled Bob driving. They didn't sing
any more. They were pretty soggy and wet. They took some
Scotch, but it had no authority against all that wind and
cold.

At last they rolled down to Casco Bay, the best duck-shoot-
ing in North America, and a camp all red-hot in the roaring
spruces, at ten o'clock. Bob's guide, part-time banker, and
boyhood friend Alphaeus had things all piping hot for them.
They thawed out at his six-foot fireplace. They steamed like
locomotives in their pants as they stood broadside to the blaze
and toasted their occidental extremities. Alph had a lobster
stew on the camp stove that smelled up all the wild night
between the wild spruces and the booming surf on the ledges.
They fell upon a ten-quart kettleful of saffron liquid with
lumps of heaven in it big as their thumbs which brought
tears to their strong eyes and flutters to their hearts. On a
wave of hot lobster stew they came back to hilarity and boy-
ishness. They let themselves out in song.

The hunters needed a more continuing heat, though, as
the lobster cooled off in them. They all thought of the Scotch.
But Bob put a finger to his lips and beckoned the York-State
boys outside. Alphaeus was a prince, he told them, between
snatches of gale, but he was also a dyed-in-wool teetotaler,
like his father, like his grandfather, like his great-grandfather
before him. They just couldn't offend his sensibilities. This
was Maine, home and shrine of Neal Dow. They would have
to go out to their car and do their drinking out there when

they got dry. The countenances of the York-State boys fell. But they all took a double swig of the Scotch and felt better. They went in.

It was all right. The boys sang all the verses of *Lydia Pinkham* they could remember, threw on another load of birch-logs. They capped one another's tall stories. The tales got taller and taller.

Bob suddenly said he had to go out to the car and refresh his memory on his wife's receipt for the biscuits he planned to bake for breakfast. Odd, but the details had slipped his mind. He took the flashlight and went out. He came back wiping his mouth with the back of his hand.

"By George!" said Bud, "do you know, I've forgot the way you make those biscuits, too. I'll have to look at that book myself." And out Bud went.

A minute later it was Jim. He had to check on them both, for he wanted those biscuits to be right.

All Alph's guests had to check up on that receipt half-a-dozen times the next two hours. Between songs and stories, they constantly found they had forgotten about the way those biscuits were built. Each time a man came back, he sang louder and thought of brawnier tales. Each time a man came back, he recalled more and more of the powerful big bags of duck, deer, and geese he had taken in his time.

Bob told about the time he first shot the family muzzle-loader. He put in seven fingers of powder, *Boston Transcript,* shot, and more *Transcript,* and he blew the whole top of the head, antlers and all, right off that moose. Bud recalled that bear he had practically strangled that Winter in the Adirondacks. Jim remembered loading his canoe so full of canvasbacks in Cayuga that it sank.

But the heat of birch-logs, the sound of wind in the spruces, and the five-hundred-mile drive had their way at last—and the constant review of the biscuit receipt. Heads sagged. Songs petered out. Bud rolled over on a bunk, coat, pants, and all. Jim dovetailed himself into Bud's contours. Bob became a mountain of snores along the hearth. Only Alph was alert. He kept an eagle eye on the embers and his wristwatch. The wind outside was going down. The hours grew smaller.

The boys had slept maybe a half minute, it seemed to them, when Alph shook them.

"Four-thirty, boys! Time to roll out! We've got to get that duck-blind built. Look alive, all hands!"

Three sleep-bound men groped for their pants and found they had them on. They stumbled out into the blackness to their guns. It was bone-cold. The air came into their warm clothes like steel knives. Numb fingers found shells and shotguns at last. The men followed Alph's flash to the dock. Alph was big as three men. He had festoons of tollers hung around him. Coots and black-duck, whittled out of Maine pine by Maine lobstermen so cunningly they looked more like wild birds than the wild birds looked themselves. The whittlers had even robbed their wives' hats to get tail-feathers to stick up saucy in their tails. The boys tumbled into the dory among the wooden decoys.

Just as Alph cast off his painter, there came a warwhoop, and a boy, so spattered with freckles you couldn't put a pin down, all ears and wide mouth in the flashlight's beam, plummeted out of the night into the boat. It was Alph's eleven-year-old hopeful. He had been in hiding for this moment all night. He wasn't going to miss this. He had a battered sixteen-gauge in his scrawny unmittened paws.

Gosh! they hadn't gotten away from children after all! Alph remonstrated. But Bill wasn't budging out of there. So Alph ran out his oars, and they went creaking out to sea.

They came up to a high island in the dark, and landed. Mostly, the boy landed. He poured out the tollers, he lifted out shells, handed out the guns. He was everywhere in the flashlight; his sharp butts worked like the hinges on scissors in and out of the boat. He did everything. He shouldered most of the strings of tollers.

Alph led the way. They teetered out on a spiny reef, slipping on the wet rockweed. Here they would build their blind, Alph said. The boys who were men were all thumbs as they picked up the stones. The boy still a boy had a breast-high wall up in five minutes. He was quick as a cat. Bob fancied himself a mason, but the boy laid up walls around him.

It was just crack of day when they finished. Alph shushed them and pointed east. A cold streak of light silvered the ocean. They crouched double in the blind. They loaded their

[67]

guns, both barrels. Alph tied stones to anchor his tollers and heaved them out, string by string. They waited an aeon. Their teeth chattered. They waited two aeons more. The coatless boy was warm as toast where he fitted Bud's thigh.

"There!" whispered Alph. A dark chevron loomed on the sky. The whistle of wings came down to them. But only a faint whistle, and it was gone. They waited some more. The cold began to shake them to their wisdom teeth.

The dawn came up like a forest fire. Suddenly the whole Atlantic Ocean was there with them. Then the sun rolled up like an ox-cart wheel out of half a world of waves. It was worth all the aches and the trouble and cold.

Ducks went by, amazing chains of them, but far off, high, and whistling like bullets. They gave the island a wide berth. Guns boomed some islands away, but the York-State guns shook cold and quiet in their owners' numbed hands. The tollers bobbed, and showed their stolen tail-feathers. But no visitors came down to call on them.

The sun was good and high when Alph gave the signal. They gathered in the tollers, or rather the boy gathered them in with about ten sweeps of the oars in his father's dory. They rowed back—that is, the boy rowed back—to the camp and breakfast.

Bob made one more trip, bolstered up by both York-State friends, to the car, and they took a last look at the receipt for those biscuits. They looked long and hard. They came back glowing and confident. Alph had three pans of biscuits turned out of the oven when they found their way into the kitchen. And there were smoking venison steaks on each man's plate. They ate like starved Indians, but no man could keep up with that mite of a boy. He seemed to have no bottom in his overalls at all. The men sat amazed and saw biscuit after biscuit go down into him. He was bottomless.

They all agreed the biscuits were as good as they could have made even if they had spent the whole night and day reading the receipt-book of Bob's talented spouse. And Alphaeus winked a twinkling eye at them, and they knew what he knew. The deermeat, smothered in butter, bacon, and onions, was incredible.

After a solid hour's eating, the gunners went out and gunned some more, for three hours. Ducks were flying all right, but they had an appointment in Spain or Africa and hugged Nova Scotia close and flew high up and fast. But the men had a lovely row in the dory, with the boy on the oars. They saw a good part of the Atlantic.

Just as they rowed home, in the low sun, something whistled overhead like a rifle bullet, the boy dropped the oars, threw up his scarred sixteen-gauge, and let go. A little bird, so high the men could not see it, came hurtling down and smacked the ocean beside them. It was a coot, about half-grown. They gathered him in.

Back home in York State, by darkened Cayuga, the people—most of the people in the village in fact—gathered for the much-advertised hunt-supper in Jim's mansion. And Mrs.

Jim marched in with her hugest platter, with game-scissors, carving tools, and everything in the way of game accessories and gear to carve up the feast, and set the platter down on the table. In the vast white space was one little lone coot, curled up brown like a small child's shoe. It was the boys' thousand-mile coot, she announced. The boys had gone that far to get it.

Outside the house legions of quacking ducks made the night loud over Cayuga.

But the next course came in. It was soup-plates high with Maine steamed clams, from Alphaeus. The next round was lobster stew, also from Alphaeus. And to top it all off, a huge Maine lobster, red as a British huntsman in his armored shell, was put down, with Alphaeus's compliments, before each bug-eyed guest. It was the hunt-supper of the century beside blue Cayuga's waters. Fish, not fowl, but a feast to be remembered a lifetime.

And no gunner in the world, vowed Bud aloud over the merrymaking, could beat that eleven-year-old Maine boy!

7. One–Man Garden

SAFE in the middle of the Winter, I like to think about my one-man garden. And I glow. But as Summer creeps nearer, I begin to grow nervous, and I do no more glowing. A garden like mine is a fine thing to look back on, but not to look ahead to. So now, in the Winter of my sweet content, exactly halfway between wrestling the last of my potatoes in and putting my first tomatoes out, I had better glow, with all the glow I can muster, about feeding myself and my friends out of my garden.

I have often sung the praises of the New England one-horse farm. There is a lot to be said for it. If nothing else, at least one gets to know the horse! There is a whole education in a horse, and if you put a harness on him and attach a cart or plow, there is almost a whole civilization. One never can really scrape up a friendship with even a single tractor, let alone a whole barnful of them. Tractors are cold, superior things. It takes an engineer even to respect them. And I am no engineer. I am a mason and a poet.

A one-horse farm is a wonderful farm for a poet to live on, and for a mason, too. The mason does not have much work to do. And the poet can find any number of poems in such hand-farming and heart-farming. It is not much head-farm-ing. Tractor farms require that. The horse, on the one-horse farm, takes the place of the head. The poet lets the horse play the part of the head naturally. The horse is much more prac-tical. The poet supplies the heart. It is the ideal co-operative farming. And besides the horse, the poet finds plenty of other things to make friends with and put into poems. With a horse to help, he has time for robins and rainbows, and quiet meditation. They are all one happy family. The horse doing the work, the robins and rainbows doing the singing and shining, and the poet resting and keeping them all in order. It is an ideal setup. It was on such a one-horse farm that I grew up and became a poet.

But that is the one-horse farm. Mine now is not that. It is merely a one-man farm. I have no horse. I have to take the place of one most of the time. And so I have to be plow and harrow, cultivator and hayrack and reaper, all in one. I have to be the whole works. I have to be the universe. Horse and cart and drag and driver, manager and all the machinery.

Of course, I have to borrow from my neighbors some things on some days—bedrock essentials. I have to borrow a horse for half a day, to plow and furrow out. But I am coming to believe I should spade up my whole garden, or dig it up with my bare hands—if my son has broken the spade in digging his angleworms for trout-fishing, as he usually has—rather than go on risking my limbs and my life and my peace of mind, with any more borrowed horses.

Now I am not the man to look a gift horse in the mouth. But there are desperate occasions when you have to do just that. And this is one of them. Three Springs ago, the horse I borrowed was blind in his off eye, and I had to lead him on the bias all the time; and my vegetables never quite got used to their biased furrows. The potatoes grew all slant-eyed and the corn slant-eared. Two Springs ago, it was a horse higher in his forequarters than his hinder parts the neighbors loaned me. As a result, the plow was always nose-diving and immobilizing itself, the horse, and me. I had to borrow an overgrown boy to perch on the plow handles to keep the plowpoint up.

But last Spring's horse was the worst. He brought me

closest to nervous prostration and the bourne from which no plowman returns. I still have the scars of my narrow escape on me. My neighbor, this time, did not think to tell me— no neighbor doing loaning ever tells you anything—that his horse had not been exercised the whole Winter long and had been hoarding up his strength for this kill. My neighbor did not tell me his horse had kicked a man some years before and ruined him. He let me discover these things for myself. I did at once. The second furrow I was doing, with another (horseless) neighbor whom I had borrowed, holding the handles of the plow I had borrowed, and me pulling the borrowed horse by the headstall by main strength, the horse danced over one tug at the turn, kicked out horizontally to all four points of the compass at once, scooched, lunged, and left for the Happy Hunting Grounds of borrowed horses.

My neighbor, a wise man, let go the plow handles at once. I couldn't let go of the horse, for I was no longer on the ground. I was swinging like a pendulum around the horse's neck, keeping time to his leaps. We were going like the wind, and the plow, also mostly in the air, was whistling like a scythe at me from behind. I knew what I was to feel if I should come loose from the horse. But by some secret super-human strength in me, I got one foot on the runaway's shoulder, gave myself an enormous push into the azure, fell clear of the plow, struck the sweet earth and stopped, and the horse disappeared, in superb bounds like a jack-rabbit's, over the horizons of far-away farms.

The plow we found on a tree, and salvaged it. We salvaged most of the harness and the whiffle-tree. We piecened things together. My neighbor was an expert piecener. And we borrowed another horse from another neighbor and went after the first. We found him. He had run the killer out of him. He had run most of his breath out, too. He was like a rag. He was gentle as a sucking dove. We brought him back to the scene of his crime, muzzled, with a pinch-bit, borrowed on our way.

We went back to the furrowing. I had been a kind man before and given the horse a rest after each furrow. But now I dragged him mercilessly on without a letup, from one furrow into the next. He wilted, but I propped him up with one thigh and kept him going. When I finally led him home, I leaned him up against the stable and left him there. For as long as I looked back, he was still there at the angle I had left him, leaning on the wall. I had taught him a lesson. It had taught me one. Next Spring, I shall run my borrowed horse five miles before I start furrowing.

You can see that the one-man farmer, like me, has to borrow a few staples besides a horse. *Item:* boys and neighbors, if you can catch them before they light out fishing; *item:* the plow, usually one of the pre-Civil-War vintage; *item:* bits of harness, as reinforcements to the original set that comes on the horse. But these are all common property. Expendables. I had most of these items once, but continuous borrowings from me have left me bare. And I repay the loan of such by the sweat of my brow and the fruits of my acres, when it comes time to hoe my neighbors' gardens for them while they take care of the baby and cheer me on, when it comes time to gather some of my crops and feed my neighbors well.

My wise neighbor, who holds the plow for my furrows, wisely lets the garden we plow up together for him, right after mine, go back to the state of nature at once, run wild to weeds, and never troubles himself about it again. He just sits and minds the baby and waits for me to bring him corn and beans. He ought to be in the United States Senate, and maybe, if I bring him enough beans, some day he will. But he is good. He loans me his baskets to bring my corn over in. It is all pure communism.

Once I have my furrows meandering up and down the slope of my plot—I am wise enough to plant on a side-hill—I spit on my hands and really begin my hand-farming. It is all by hand from there on, to the last cabbage dragged from the November snows.

As I used to do when I was a boy mowing with a man's scythe, I generally bite off more than I can chew. I like my garden to be about the size of my barn. It is an old New England rule. But as my barn is one of the old Homeric Age, when every farmer worth his salt begot twelve boys, it is a twelve-boy barn. (You don't count the girls.) And so my garden plot runs to over half an acre.

I say goodbye to house and children. And of course my friends keep warily away. I put on my second-best shoes and my third-best pants. I go out into the great Outdoors. And I live there, under the mark of Cain, from the first bluets to the last frosts. I aim to get my seeds all in by Decoration Day. This may sound late, but this is Maine and on the edge of the Arctic. The frosts of early June are almost as bad as those of early September. And, anyway, three months at hard labor is enough for any man.

I use commercial fertilizer. Yet I am not above borrowing the barn or hen dressing of neighbors, for the vegetables I really pamper, on the dark nights, or when they are at the movies or looking the other way. This is no theft but thrift. They do the same by my cucumbers when I am hard at a sonnet. I fertilize the rows, drop all the seeds, and cover them all in by hand. I play no favorites. I plant everything. I rush in where angels would fear to tread, and try cabbages. From radishes that need nothing but a fissure, to kidney beans that have to be handled with kid gloves, and warmed by my hands in a fog, I try them all.

Potatoes are my chief money crop and my pride. They are what my neighbors count on most. I have a way of cutting them up, so that two eyes of their skins face the south, that no one has ever improved on. Maine, of course, is the world's best potato soil, and I, on my modest scale, am one of the world's artists at them. Or so my neighbors say. They egg me on. They stand by and applaud when I hoe, poison, hoe, poison, hoe, poison, educate, and dig them. There is no one like me at potatoes, they swear. I use three kinds of poison, to make sure I get the right one, put it on with the brush I use on my Sunday pants, and end up—and it is end-up!—by picking the bugs off by hand and immersing them in kerosene, as I did when a boy. Only no one pays me the old five-cents-a-cup rate. I dig the potatoes just as the borers uncoil, on the full of the September moon, and reject every flawed one. I am proud of my twenty-two bushels of Maine's seventy-six-million-bushel crop.

Kidney beans, though, are my masterpiece. My soil is clay and slopes to the ocean. The fogs are a perpetual menace, but my beans love to look out to sea. And something of the savor of the sea gets into them if you hoe them only on the flood tide and never allow a hand to touch them on hazy days; and they are something to sing about when they are poured singing from the bean pot. But between the first sprouts and the miracles of Saturday night there is constant labor, and love. I bring them up by hand, hill them up by hand, for fear steel touch them, pull them, stack them, dry them. And then my children have hours of work shelling them out in the barn. But my barn is a noble place to be, higher than a church, and one has noble thoughts there, and, anyway, my children love beans! Because my kidney beans taste of sea, I have more good friends on Saturday nights than on any three other nights of the year.

I am a poet as well as a farmer, remember. So I don't leave aesthetics out of my garden. I put flowers right in with the vegetables. Generally, save with potatoes and corn, which are clannish vegetables and get lonely in separated rows, I put a row of flowers in between the rows of vegetables. My nasturtiums are notorious. It is the salt in the air, I fancy. Anyway, they run like wildfire up and down the rows, and strong men, after the third day they begin to blossom, could not keep them picked even though they gathered them by the wash tub. My bachelor-buttons become a blue wilderness, and children have been known to get lost in my cosmos and have to be tracked down by search parties. I have zinnias also, like great rosettes of bronze. I even dare sweet-peas and come off with flying colors. I fence the entire garden in with sunflowers. They stand guard with their faces to sea winds and keep them from getting at my beans, and they keep the witchgrass out with their roots. If I had a horse to cultivate my rows, I should have to sacrifice these big-eyed Guardsmen. Knowing my neighbors' horses as I do, I much prefer my sunflowers.

My morning-glories are what I am most famed for among flowers. The Kentucky heavenly-blues were never so blue or so big in the bluegrass, I swear. And spiraling up the white-birch poles I stick for them, they are a sight to see of an August morning. One Summer, I had seven hundred of these seraphs looking at me wide-eyed at once, when I was up with the robins at sunrise. I shall carry that sight with me, I hope, when my sight forever fails.

I see a good deal of my morning-glories because I see a good deal of the mornings. My feet are parboiled all the Summer months with the dew. For I have to be up early. I wage an endless war on the woodchucks. They live under my huge old barn, and they eat off all the rows of my peas nearest the barn every morning, unless I am there doing sentry-go. I have used up all my twenty-two cartridges on them years ago. So I have to fight with my bare hands and my voice. My woodchucks are wiser than the Indians. They post sentries. They know which window in the house is mine. They know when I have got on my pants. By the time I get to the garden, they are all fast asleep, full of my young peas, in the bosom of their families, under the tie-up. There are hundreds of them, I think, and like most Maine farmers, they send many of their sons to college. That is why they are such scientists at destroying me and my hopes in the Summer.

Crows are pretty shrewd enemies of mine, too. But I have the Maine farmers' antidote for them. I string strings of twine up and down my hills of corn. The black thieves are more afraid of these than of any number of their cousins, hung up dead, head down, with spread wings. It puzzles them deeply. They sit all over my elms and try to figure it out.

But my neighbors' cows and heifers and goats and pigs and hens are my worst foes. I have no fences. My neighbors have none. So at any breakfast, I may look out and see all these animals and birds having a Democratic Presidential Convention right in the middle of my corn. I rush out and chase them into all the woods in three directions, and into the sea at the other. This year, I made good the havoc a neighbor's goats wrought by putting them all into a poem, and getting paid folding money for it. Being a poet comes in handy on a farm.

Two vegetables I raise furnish the family with two of our best Summer dinners. String-beans and green-corn. We cook the beans in the old family kettle, and with a half pound of fat, salt pork nested in their midst. We cook them three hours on a slow fire of beech wood. They are the whole dinner. String-beans aren't just vegetables, cooked this way; they are the soup, fish, the entree, and roast. When they are snapped and cooked fresh from their vines this way, and the windows of our house are open, the neighbors become excited. They feign excuses to come over at high noon, with a cup of sugar they borrowed years ago, or a rake or a baby-buggy of mine which they discover they have had for decades. They hang around, and their tongues hang out, and their mouths water. But there is enough of our dish for a dozen neighbors. We spin out a few plates and dish out the beans.

Our green-corn is another pinnacle of the Summer. Especially the first mess. The day it comes in outranks any child's birthday. I watch the ears like a hawk. One fine forenoon, the silk on some of them droops, browned ever so little. I break off those ears and run bee-line for the house, shouting. The people there hear my shouts and start the kettle boiling. I husk the ears between woodshed and kitchen, the water is boiling when I get them to the kettle, and I drop them in. In an eye's twinkle they are transfigured. The milk in the beads along the cobs turns into a cross between honey and manna. We dish the ears out and smear on the butter. We close our eyes and eat from left to right, as the typewriter travels, clockwise, two rows of honey-*cum*-butter beads at a time. Maybe it is ten minutes, not more, from the cornstalk to the stomach. And the stomach puts on wings! When I bite into green-corn from my clay, I forget all the weeks of sweat and tears and blisters behind me. I forget hot July hours I hoed with only a big rhubarb leaf between my brain and sunstroke. I burgeon like the buds of Spring. It was worth all the pains and more.

Yet the greatest virtue of one-man gardening, the gardening of the amateur, is this: It makes you, in spite of all the dubious tools and horses and boys the neighbors have lent you, in spite of short-sighted advice they have lavished upon you, a better neighbor. For when, at the year's golden end, your cornucopia runs over, and you wheel in more wheelbarrows of beets and carrots and squashes than you and the few children left on the roost could eat in ten Winters, you keep right on past your barn, around the corner of the house, and to your neighbor's yard. And there, among his babies on the lawn and assorted dogs, you roll out your jewels to give away. And you go home feeling like the Golden Rule.

Giving vegetables away makes one-man gardening the best avocation on this round, green earth.

II

MAINE FAMILY
ON THE GO

8. An American for a Father

MY FATHER was the kind every American boy ought to
have. He was an all-round man. He could whittle out a
boat for a small boy and build one for a big one to row in. He
sailed a sloop of his building all his life. He could rig a sail,
but he could break a colt and teach a boy manners, too. He
could ride a horse or swop one, shoot wild geese and shel-
drakes. But he could make good hay and raise fine potatoes

just as well. He told stories, drew pictures, sang songs. He built houses and good soil and strong children. He did many things at the same time, and all over. He had friends on every road. He was his own boss. He was a three-ring circus, with every ring going at once. He was young as his youngest boy. He was a daisy!

My father was a handsome man, to begin with, and handsomeness is a good thing for a boy to grow up to, especially if he is all ears and jaws and sharp corners as I was. My father was big-built. He was only five-foot-nine, as I have discovered lately, but he made up in width what he lacked in length. He took the largest sizes in everything. Square was the word for him. He was square all over, from his curly head to the toes of his cowhides. His head had high corners to it. His bumps of ideality, as he himself might have put it when he got on his favorite subject of phrenology, were large. He had wide hands and knees that were broad and comfortable for a small boy to ride on at night.

This first man I knew was built like his own oxen, and he always seemed to be leaning his strength against something. He could pick up great stones or lift a barrel of flour in his two hands. And he needed to, for there were so many of us children to feed that he had a lot of flour to lift, and he brought it home by a dozen barrels at a time. As I remember him, he was always working. It was his favorite recreation. My first memory of him is seeing him building our house from the inside. He had an aureole of sawdust around his hair; he was sawing out laths and drowning out the sound his saw made with a hymn tune he was singing:

> I love the sound of Jesus' name,
> It sets my spirit all into flame,
> Glory to the bleeding Lamb!

My father loved the downright Moody and Sankey hymns. He always sang them while he was working. They were the best tunes to work by, he said. *Hold the Fort* and *Only an Armor-Bearer.* Songs with strong men in them. He liked the kind of religion that had, as he put it, "muscle and guts to it."

My father was built solid, too. Like his religion. When he stepped on a furrow, the furrow gave and broke wide under him. When he got into a skiff, that skiff knew it had a load; it creaked in its boards and went well down in the water. He was hefty and broad in the beam. When he rocked in his rocking-chair, nights, we heard him all through the house. He worked even then. He rocked right across the kitchen, got up chair and all, turned around, and came rocking right on back.

The moustache my father wore was the gates-ajar kind. But his was thicker and had more golden fire in it than any my uncles had. And it turned up at the ends and made my father look as if he was always smiling. He generally was, too. My father was the smiling kind.

[87]

My father was good-looking because he had been out in the weather all his life. If you put even a homely man out in the rain and the sun for fifty years, he will turn into a handsome man. And my father was probably good-looking to start with. His skin was the color of acorns. And he had the Maine blue eyes, the kind that come from being out in sea-scud and looking sharp at important things like reefs and fog banks a long ways off. Far-away blue, they were—deep but very bright at the same time. My father came by his eyes honestly, going and coming between the islands he owned, in his dory or schooner, many years. And the wind had crinkled up the skin at the corners of his eyes, so that made him look as though he was always laughing, too. And laughing is a good thing for boys to see a father do. Especially when they have just broken his best axe-helve, as we often had!

This man who was responsible for me was self-made, like the best Americans. He began working when he began to walk. And he had no time to go to school; he was too busy living. So as a boy he read his books at night, after he had worked a man's long day in a cotton mill. He found time for reading all right. He cut it out of sleep. He read on his belly in front of the kitchen fireplace, the way Lincoln and the other pioneers read. He educated himself while he was resting. And because he made reading his resting, he never stopped reading when he grew up. He kept right on with books. He got a little time off in the Civil War. When he was laid up in a hospital in Virginia, he picked up his Latin. He found an interlinear translation of the *Aeneid* near his cot, and he read it clean through. He learned his Latin that way. I still have that Virgil. I learned my Latin out of it, too, at nine, before the teachers got at me, all by myself.

My father never stopped learning. He was what he would call "a well-posted man." He kept up with the world by newspapers and magazines as well as books. He always took four or five newspapers. He took the *Missouri Valley Farmer* away up in Maine, halfway to the North Pole! He was well up in history, geography, astronomy, navigation, politics, and agriculture. History was a favorite with him. He liked any books that had big men in them. Napoleon for one. He was an authority on Napoleon. He had a fellow feeling for him. He had his life in seven volumes. I recall an old song he used to sing about bringing back the bones of Bonaparte from St. Helena.

My father had a large library, for a farmer and a fisherman. About two thousand volumes. He had the unexpurgated *Arabian Nights*. I used to read that under the parlor sofa. Nobody knew about that but my father, and he laughed and said nothing. Father had Doré's Dante, too, and Doré's La Fontaine and *Paradise Lost*. He liked Doré's downright black-and-whites. He had a deep feeling for Milton. But he had just as deep a feeling for Shakespeare, too. He used to read Shakespeare to me from the time I was six and understood only words here and there. He would let himself rear up and go when he got into the kings' parts. He would toss his curls like a king and snort and shout. I loved that. My father could say a lot of speeches without the book. He was fascinated by anatomy, too. He had a medical encyclopedia, and it had a whole map of the human body, on different levels. You kept going deeper and deeper. It got more interesting as it went in. I loved that also. I used to pore over it under the sofa, too. When my mother came into the room suddenly, I would have to shut the big volume quick, and some of the organs of the Anatomized Man were bound to be left sticking out of the pages. My father knew about my reading that book also. He laughed some more.

Books were one part of his education, but my father had learned most of what he knew by living hard and working at many kinds of trades outdoors. Fishing, farming, carpentering, boat-building. It did not matter what it was, so long as he was his own boss and carved out his own way with his two gnarled hands. For my father was a pioneer. It might strike you as strange to find a pioneer in a settled part of America, at this late day. But there my father was, living like Dan'l Boone and George Rogers Clark and Nimrod and Esau. There he was, going right through early American history all over again, taming the wild, making it blossom, filling it with children. Then, when neighbors moved in too close, he pulled up stakes and went and found a new promised land with plenty of elbow room, cleared out the trees and built his house all over again.

There was plenty virgin soil to open to the sun in my father's time, in Maine. Below his town was Casco Bay with a hundred islands that only herons and deer had inhabited before my father came. My father picked out the wildest and loneliest ones. And pretty soon there would be a cradle, too, with a baby in it, being sung to sleep by the spruces. My father's idea of a good home was one that took a lot of pains to get to. I don't know as I have ever found a better definition for a good one.

Spruce Island was a fair sample of my father's turning wilderness to civilization. My father went there when he had babies that could only creep or waddle. His first night on the island, he slept over a fire he had lit in his clearing. As he dozed there, a huge eagle swooped down out of the night, seized a blazing brand out of the heart of the fire, and flew off with it in his claws, screaming and scattering red sparks through the forest. But eagles and coals of fire in the woods could not scare my father away.

The only neighbors my father had were often bobcats and owls. One morning when he was walking bright and early to town, he saw a great *loup-cervier* creeping on his belly ahead of him, stalking a bewhiskered old farmer who was driving his yoke of oxen and minding his own business. My father picked up two stones and ran at the panther. He let out a yell. The big cat turned and flowed up over a stonewall and away into the woods as soundless as a squirrel, quick as you could wink an eyelash. When the old farmer turned, he saw my father running with the stones in his hands, and he put the goad into his oxen and lit out for glory. He thought my father had gone crazy and was coming to kill him. Though my father explained it all afterwards, the old fellow always kept a weather eye on him and never felt relaxed in his company.

One night when my mother was going to the hen-pen to gather in her eggs by lantern light, an eagle attacked her with tearing claws and lashing wings. She had to drop her light and run for dear life. That was the kind of island Spruce Island was.

My father drove his yoke of oxen to that island over four miles of bay ice. Once his oxen went through, and he lost both of them out of the yoke in the dark, before he could set them free and get them back on the ice. Life was hard sledding, but he made it. He ran two stores in town, built barns, plowed up new acres for beans and corn, fished a hundred lobster traps, seined mackerel and shad, built his own boats, and begot more children. The only time he ever got scared was in a season when talk of a sea-serpent was going the rounds. My father was out pulling his lobster traps in the fog, at dusking time, and a long cold tentacle came out of the mist and wrapped itself around his neck. His first gray hairs, he said, came that night. He tore the slimy living thing off. It was a twenty-foot ribbon of kelp swinging from a spar he had drifted up to in the gloom.

Mother lived nights and days and weeks alone, with only

sheep to hear besides the surf, with croupy children and no neighbors nearer than a lantern's shine across miles of wild water. She had cows to milk and bed down, wood to get, fires to make, a hundred chores to do besides her cooking. But she loved it. And the children flourished. Mother doctored them and taught them to read—and collected her money as a school teacher later from the town! She had a fine time. It was the happiest time of her life.

When it came time for my father to move on to a new wilderness, and he gave the deed to Spruce Island to its new owner, he went out to the stonewall he had built around his pasture and took out his bank from between two stones. It was an earthen crock, and it had two thousand silver dollars in it. My father liked silver money. He knew he was holding money when he held it in silver cartwheels. And he liked to bank in the open all his life. He had amassed that much of his fortune in the five years he had owned Spruce Island. He had earned it all with his bare hands, his bright plow, and his lobster traps.

The next island in the family was the one I cut my first teeth on. It was State of Maine granite and a fine island to cut teeth on. It was the last island out between Maine and Spain. My father ran up a new house there, out of ships' timbers that had washed ashore. It was so windy there wasn't a tree on the whole island. My father had to anchor his house down with two ox chains over the ridgepole. When the wind changed, he had to go out in his night-tails and shift the chains! I learned to creep on the ledges of Pond Island. I caught my first cunner there and tumbled into the Atlantic in ecstasy. But my father was on hand and pulled me right out. He was always on hand.

When it got too cold and stormy to live on that island, my father brought his schooner up to the side of the house, pushed the house and us in it on to the deck, and took us up and planted us on an island nearer the mainland. It was wilderness, though, and we heard lynxes howling at night when we rowed over the bay, coming home from the red-brick country schoolhouse we got our education in. In Winter, we had to walk home across the bay ice. We all carried long pine poles, to hold us up when we broke through, and we went Indian file, with the leading boy trying the ice with his axe. It was the best schooling I ever had.

Don't let people tell you America is filled up now, and there is no more pioneering to do. There is more wilderness to tame in Maine now than there was two hundred years ago. New Hampshire and Vermont are full of abandoned places where men can start all over new. You come up and see. There is plenty room for a man like my father, a man who loves to build his life with his two hands. America is full of room for Americans.

It was a fine thing to talk and walk and ride and work with a man who was making American history. That was what my father was doing. He was a man out of the sagas the ancient poets used to sing. He was a man who started with only his strength and ended up as head of a clan. My father had been in the Civil War and taken part in events like those in the *Old Testament.* He had taken part in that epic within our history, that cussedest and yet most colorful and civilest civil war of all, when cavalry charged gunboats and took them, when enemies swopped songs over the picket lines at night, when Stonewall Jackson and Little Mac rode out like Gideons at the head of armies of men who loved them as sons love a father. My father had carried his best friend out of battle with his friend's leg bones sticking out white through his trouser legs. He had talked and swopped jokes with Lincoln in a hospital bed. I still have the photograph Lincoln gave him. He had been sent home weighing only about ninety pounds. But he had cheated the doctors, got up on his pins, opened up an oyster shop, got himself a wife and raised a family. He raised his family on a place he had cleared in the forest, just as the first settlers in America had raised theirs.

Our family was his second go. We children were his second set. There were ten of us in this batch. It sounds like something from the *Old Testament,* but it was so. Our father trained us to grow up smart and be somebody. He taught all of us boys a trade. One brother of mine became the boat-builder of the family, another the family carpenter. I was trained as the mason. I have chimneys and walls to my credit. My wife used to be sorry I could not drive a nail straight. For a carpenter comes in handier around a house than a stone-mason. But when she wanted a fireplace laid up, I was always her man.

Just to be on the safe side, in case we might not make our

own way, my father built each child of us a house. Ten houses. With his own hammer and saw and square. We have never needed those houses, for we have earned too many of our own for our own children. He might have known we would take after him.

By the way, when I counted them five years ago, my mother had twenty-eight grandchildren. No one of us has come up to our father, as yet. He had fourteen children, counting both sets. But some of us have done fairly well by the future.

My father was an American father because he worked with his hands as well as his head. Most American fathers do. No matter what railroads or houses or banks they acquire, they like to strip off their coats and do things with their fingers for themselves. Thomas Jefferson was that kind of man. He filled his palatial Monticello with gadgets which he built for himself, for bringing things up from the cellar and cooling his drink. This gentleman who uses his hands in labor is something new in civilization. He is the American gentleman. He is near enough to pioneer days to want to carry his own things, use his own tools, build his own bookcases, hoe his own rows.

The father I had worked harder than any of his hired-men. He had a lot of hired-men around, but he led the way with his pitchfork in the hayfield and with his hammer on the roof of a barn he was putting up. He loved to quote his favorite philosopher in the great American School of Experi-

ence, Ben Franklin: "If you'd have it done, go; if not, send."
He was always quoting Poor Richard. Carpenter, hayer,
stone-mason, shopkeeper, business man, he was also a fisherman and made his own gear and tarred his own nets. He
loved white paint passionately, and he put it on everything.
Even the bailers in his boats were painted white, as well as
his lobster buoys. Father was a king whittler in a region
noted for whittling. He made wooden coots that looked
more alive and smiling than the real coots. He carved his
name with a flourish on everything he owned, boat-seats,
lobster buoys, shovel-handles, pitchforks. He put a flourish
on all he touched. He had a lot of work to his name in his
sixty-odd years. He shingled a hundred roofs, hoed tens of
thousands of turnips, built and fished hundreds of lobster
pots, and plowed scores of fields.

But my father had just as many friends as he had turnips
and lobster traps. Friends were a chief crop with him. He
learned more from them than he learned from his many
books. He made all kinds. He knew everybody, big-wigs
and little-wigs. General Joshua L. Chamberlain, hero of
Little Round Top at Gettysburg, President of Bowdoin, and
Governor of Maine, was his best friend; so were Senators and
men high in law and medicine. But my father also knew
plain fishermen and farmers who had never been very far
away from their herring nets and their kidney beans. His
store, built right into the bridge that connected one of his
islands with the mainland, was the place where he parceled

out philosophy and wisdom, as well as all kinds of sea-food
and fish-hooks and boats. He met his friends there. They
came from all over New England and far beyond to hear my
father talk and tell stories and settle the problems of history
along with those of seining smelts. He would sit up all night
to talk. I learned to sit up all night with him. This store of
his became a famous place. In it hundreds of Americans
heard human nature in full cry, and smiling as it cried. My
father could make graybeards sit up starry-eyed. He knew
history because he had walked through it, in the Civil War
and out. He knew medicine because he had doctored his
children. He knew astronomy by living out so much with
the stars. And he had learned how to be wise among small,
ordinary people making a living with their shoulders and
thighs. He found some good to say of even the rascals. A
thief might have a good baritone voice.

Though he was a democrat through and through, my
father was a rock-ribbed Republican. A Democrat was someone to be pitied, like an underwitted child, as he put it. He
hated a Copperhead as he hated dirt and laziness. Southern-
ers were always Rebs to him, although he called them Rebs
with a smile. The only man he hated in the whole Civil War
was the lieutenant in his company who let him go without a
shirt through a Virginia Winter. He held hardness against
this one man alive, and one day when, as it was bound to
happen sooner or later, this man came into the store on the
bridge, he got no wisdom or fish-hooks. He got a left to the

ear and a right to the mouth, and when he came to, he had to be husbanded into his buggy by the bystanders.

My father was usually in the thick of Republican rallies, wherever the torchlights sputtered the hottest. He was a power in politics. He named a son for Benjamin Harrison. He would have gone on naming sons for Republican Presidents, but unfortunately the line ran out. So when I came along, I had to be named after a mere ancestor, the first Coffin in America, who bred Nantucket Island its best whalers. My father tried to name a son after his friend Joshua Chamberlain. But my mother put her foot down at that. Joshua was too much. We compromised by naming our current pet goose after the Civil War General who received Lee's sword of surrender.

And when Teddy Roosevelt came along, my father worshipped him so ardently that he wanted to name a son for him, too. He never got over his disappointment when he was not allowed to. We children christened our pet eagle Teddy Roosevelt, to help lessen my father's grief. My father subscribed most heartily to T.R.'s idea of a big family. He had been practicing it for years. His bump of philoprogenitiveness, as he said when he was reading bumps on his own head, was great. A good family was a long table lined with children both sides. He subscribed to T.R.'s ideal of the strenuous life also. Up to his heart in lobsters or his bees, he vowed happiness was keeping busy. Teddy was a man after his own heart. He was sorry he could not claim him as his own son.

The man I had for father liked a lot of things hard. He liked the humor of Mark Twain hard, in a New England that still looked down its nose at the crude Westerner. He liked his American heartiness, and he introduced me to Twain's immortal boys, Huck and Tom, the minute the long ringlets were off my square head and my legs had got out of skirts and into breeches. My father liked a fast horse, even when his curls flew white as snow in the wind. He liked the first airplanes he saw, and prophesied we would all be traveling in them some day. He liked to leave his two-for-five Porto Rico Crook cigars around where a son of seven might find them and toughen himself up for a life of smoking ahead. Best of all, my father loved a new baby boy and ached for the day when the boy would be big enough to ride on his knee and be told stories.

This father of mine liked *Paradise Lost,* but he liked good food just as well. Good eating was one of his passions. Here again he loved the downrights—tripe, raw oysters, salt-dried-cod in chunks. He would cut up a whole fish with his jack-knife and eat it while driving to town, feeding slabs to his boys on the knife's point. But he loved eels smothered, a ham smoked by his own popple wood, and Kennebec turkeys taken all aflame out from under the cookstove's cover by the tail. These roasted herring had a flavor that bit, and that was why he liked them so. His pockets were stuffed out with strong cheese for him and us, his girls and boys. He could eat a five-pound calf's-head cheese at a sitting. He liked his eggs fried hard.

He was an expert cook himself. He invented dishes of his own. One of them still runs in our family. Each new wife we acquire has to learn it. It is chicken dumplings. You cut up and cook your chicken with onions and plenty of water. Then you make what might have become piecrust on a pie for an angel; roll it wafer-thin with a bottle; slash it into rectangles; and, while the soup is still boiling, drop them tenderly in, one at a time; let each cook till it drowns; put the kettle on the back of the stove; and let nature do its subtle work for fifteen minutes. The dumplings come out with all the chicken flavor in them, they melt away at the touch of the tongue, and you taste what heaven is going to be like if you ever get there!

This man could run up a cod's-head chowder that put the sun into a cloudy day. He caught the cod himself, hove out the pioneer iron kettle he always carried in his boat, put it on his fire, threw in chunks of the salt pork he also always carried in his boat, fried it into a blue fog, threw in onions and burned them till they squirmed brown, cut up his fish while they were still flopping, threw them in heads and all, let them burn on a bit, doused in water, boiled the mess hard till it rose up over the kettle and put out the fire. Then he put in milk, made crude pioneer spoons out of clamshells shoved into split sticks, set the kettle down and let us fall to. Beulah Land! I can taste that chowder yet! My father was best at his cooking outdoors. He needed the whole Atlantic around him. He could cook lobsters and clams so that the northwest wind, the blue sky, the fierce sunlight, and the salt and iodine of the ocean got cooked right into the creatures in shells. My father loved to eat all the meals he could in the open. He was a pioneer to the end of his days. My mother had to serve her dinners in Summertime out on a table he had built her under the hemlocks. Ants and bees got into the food. But food never tasted better.

Between tons of turnips he raised and tons of lobsters he handled, between colts and boys he broke and brought up, my father found time even to be an artist. He painted signs for his shops, posters for rallies, pictures for his friends and of his friends. He put the fish and men he knew so well on paper and canvas. He had saved the reason of lonely and sick soldiers in his war by drawing lusty pictures that made them glad to be among the living. He went on the rest of his life doing that. He painted Horace Greeley, who advised men to go west, getting the boot for going Down East to Maine to seek political advancement. The men he drew were four-square and solid-built like himself. He painted whales and swordfish and turnips that ran on men's legs and smiled. He made them all into people.

My father liked people because he *was* people and loved life. Life was his business wherever he found it shining. His talk was the sound people make when they open their lips in excitement. It was full of proverbs, pungent and sharp ones. A thin meal was a dinner of "wind-pudding." A man who was shiftless was "no more use than a last year's crow's nest." My father liked to take pride down a peg or two, take the wind out of big-bellied sails, bring up with a round turn a man who was "head up and tail over the dashboard." He liked to make arrogant men "laugh out of the other corner of their mouth." My father's speech was full of the color of life. A man who got hanged "danced the hornpipe on nothing." A man who was old and feeble had "one foot in the grave and the other all butter." A quick rain was like "sheep trotting over a roadway." A homely man had a face "like a basket of eels." My father liked men who were "thick through the pants"—that was how he put it. He liked men who were good breeders, "good roosters, roosters with authority." His own philoprogenitiveness, remember, was large. He made up proverbs and folk idioms for himself, as Shakespeare did. He had no use for a man who let his wife "wear the pants." There was a man in our neighborhood who did, and my father called him and his wife, "Uncle Nance and Aunt Peter." A man without children was a "half-bottomed man," and for him there was no cure.

One of the best poems I have ever come across was my father's description of the sad-sounding south wind. He said it came around the eaves and cried, "No pork and no molasses!" Pork and molasses are the staples of New England living. When they are gone, then you are down to the dregs of despair.

My father summed up his whole American philosophy of honest labor in the worst word he could use on a man. He said it with a hiss. "Eye-servant!" It was the worst he could say of anyone. A man who worked only when somebody's eye was on him was utterly lost.

In his earlier days, my father had been a teetotaler, but he had got over that and grown wiser by the time I got acquainted with him. He did not believe that my schoolbook, *A Healthy Body,* told the truth when it pictured the apocalyptic things which one small drink of whisky did to the liver and the stomach. He vowed his own insides would have been completely galvanized if that were so. He drank whisky when he needed it, and he was sure his liver liked it, too, and did not turn into the forest fire my book described. A bonfire, maybe, but a bonfire is good on a frosty night!

What my father said about my Aunt Margaret's cold-cure was a poem, too, a piece out of a saga. That cold-cure was called *Composition*. It was made out of all the peppers, red, black, and cayenne. It was camouflaged with bayberry, and mixed with hot milk. But when we drank it at the stairs' foot, we did so with trepidation in our vitals; we drank it all at one gulp, and ran upstairs with tears welling fiercely from our eyes. The cold that could withstand its arrival inside us was a cold to be respected. My father had the right name for that remedy. It was "a red-hot torchlight procession!"

To me, my father meant more in the way of education than any other human being or college I have come upon. I was cut out to be a poet, I think, from the beginning, and my father was keen enough to see that and show me how.

He taught me to love life, in books and people and woods and waters. Though he trained me as the mason of the family, to lay up stone, he knew from the start that I was to be the book-man among his children. So he gave me the key to his library. He gave me his books themselves, one set after another, as I grew up to each. He gave me his prized Napoleon, his Henry Clay, his life of Daniel Webster. He let me bury my head and read straight through days and weeks at a time, and did my chores for me. My brothers often were angry. They twitted me with being the "white hen's chicken." But my father stood up to them and fended them off. Like John Milton's father, he gave instructions that I was to be allowed to burn the lamp as late at night as I wanted to. Aunt Margaret was the only one who dared to blow a lamp out on me. She was my father's sister and was older than he was, so she dared to do it. But when she wasn't around, I often read until the roosters crew. My father took great pride in my achievements at school.

But I learned more from my father's stories than I learned from books. I spent half of my time, up till I was seven or eight, on his knee, whenever he was resting, learning to draw pictures or learning what had made my father the man he was. I learned American history there and the American philosophy of each tub's standing on its own bottom. I learned about Hannibal and John Paul Jones and what goes into the making of a strong man. I learned about ghosts and Indians also, for my father was up on them, too. He was the best story-teller I have ever heard. His stories stay with me still.

And, best of all, I went out into the sunlight and the night and learned about the whole wide flow of life with my father pointing out the beauty in it all. He taught me to read the weather in pine needles and clouds, the years in the trunk of an oak. He schooled me in the tides and the language of the bird tracks on the snow. I learned about the pride a man has in having sons by pulling my end of a cross-cut saw in an oak log with my father pulling his end and telling me about the kind of sons I ought to have. I found out about the love of all fathers one night when I was a small boy and very ill and was lying in my room in the dark. My father came in and lit a match and leaned over me with the match in his hands, and his worried face became the loveliest poem I have ever seen.

And another night with my father became a part of me. He and I had been cutting the junipers out of the pasture, and burning them on a ledge. It was March, and it was cold. When it came on dark, my father swept the ashes off the ledge and spread down his blanket on the stone. The ledge was still holding the heat of the fire. We lay down together on it. The fire came up out of the rock and into our bodies all night long. My father put his arms around me, for I was still small enough for him to do that. I thought about how much he knew about a ledge's holding fire that way. It was something he must have learned from the Indians or the pioneers. After a while, I went to sleep, curled up in my father's arms. And I dreamed that my father's arms had become the starry skies themselves and held me and all things up in space. I knew for sure, then, I was going to be a poet.

Turnips were my father's specialty in his latter years, when I made his acquaintance. He raised thirty tons of them each year. He had a secret fertilizer, and he never let his neighbors find out what it was. It was the only thing, I guess, he ever failed to share with his neighbors. It was mussel-mud. He dug it up out of the bay at low tide in the Winter and hauled it by the horse-sled and spread it on his snow-covered field. It was dark blue and had myriads of the azure, double wings of bygone mussels in it. The thaws sweetened it and worked it into the earth. The neighbors spied on him, but they never found out what made our turnips grow so big and smooth.

I handled every turnip of ours five or six times. I transplanted them, I thinned them out, I hoed them, I watered them, I drove grasshoppers off them, I pulled them and cut off their tops, I lugged them to the shore and rolled them down the chute into our gunlow. I helped row them across the bay, I helped lug them out at the store, helped trim them and wash them and bag them, and take them to market. I had a good time. My father insisted on washing them. It was one of his extra touches that made him the successful farmer he was. He sat over a tub in the cold November night and scrubbed each last rutabaga with a burlap rag. Then, as his last flourish, he trimmed off each stem into a perfect square with diagonals coming up to a point. It was his Solomon's seal of perfection.

That was my father's secret, the American secret. He made thrift an adventure and hard work a play. He was up to his middle in work day and night and made it so breathless a thing that we children wanted to work like him. He might have to bribe us younger ones at first, paying us five cents a cupful for potato-bugs we picked off the vines, a cent a row for turnips we thinned out. But we wound up by falling in love with work and not being able to tell where play left off and work began. We got so we confused the two things. To this day we children of his do. We keep busy most of our time. We do ten things at once. I keep three books going along with two houses and farms. I teach and write together. I keep contented by working hard. In after hours. That is when work is pleasantest. A few years ago, my wife made me take a day off, without writing a word or thinking a thing. It was the hardest day I ever put in. At sunset, I gave up, rushed to my desk, and saved what sanity I had left.

Our father taught us life by living it and letting us live it with him. Everywhere he went, he was up to his elbows and heart in bright-eyed girls and boys. He let us sit on the roof and hand him his nails when he shingled, even though some of us were so small we might swallow a few nails, and did. He let us help yank in the codfish he had hooked on his line. He let us pitch hay with him and chase after the whistler he had winged. He loved to have a wagon-load of us when he drove home at all hours of the night. He kept us up late and got us up early. We learned to know the stars and the sunrise by riding beside him through them. We came home under the Northern Lights and the morning stars, singing together.

When he felt his age on him, my father knocked off work long enough to travel to the four corners of America. He hankered to see it all. He looked at the Grand Canyon, the redwoods, Puget Sound, Los Angeles, the deserts, the Mississippi, the Southern plantations. He talked and joked with men in most of the states. He saw America built up and thriving now. But he saw nothing new. He had been building this America all his life. He had harnessed tides and felled trees and built houses. He had peopled the forests with children. He was at home wherever men had worked hard and got ahead. He was at home among Americans.

He came home and harnessed up his mare and drove back to his farms and his work. He drove his mare right up to the edge of the grave.

My father had done well by life. He had been farmer, sailor, boat-maker, fisherman, reader, country gentleman, hunter, thinker, philosopher-at-large, believer in life, lover of life, a builder of soil and men. He had earned his rest. He had helped make our land what it is: A place where a common hard-working man walks like a king.

9. Yuletide on Uncle Thomas

IT was the handsomest Christmas we boys ever spent, that one we spent on our Uncle Thomas. Our mothers did not approve; our fathers didn't. And Uncle Thomas' wife, my Aunt Elda, did not, especially. But Uncle Thomas did.

When I say we boys of our family, and of ones adjoining ours in blood, spent the red-and-green holiday on Uncle Thomas, I mean that. For I am speaking as one with the

sea in his blood should speak. Uncle Thomas was a sea captain, and spending Christmas on him means spending Christmas on board his vessel.

Not that my sea-going uncle wasn't man enough to hold
most of us boys—since most of us were in very brief breeches—
on his voluminous person. He was. He was built like a
chunky coastal schooner himself. He was broad at the stern
and blunt at the stem. And he was generous amidship. I
spent many of the happiest hours of childhood exploring his
hull and walking his gang-planks. He didn't mind small
children walking and sitting all over his decks. Yes, Uncle
Thomas was a big man. He had big moustaches, a big square
back, and a broad mind. That was why he wanted us boys
on him for this particular Yuletide, when most of our uncles
would have liked to see us in Timbuktu, or even Tophet.

Now going aboard Uncle Thomas did not mean going far
from home. Not at Christmas time. Uncle Thomas was not
as far from my Lost Paradise Farm as my Aunt Elda, the wife
of his bosom, was. He was about five hundred yards nearer,
as a matter of fact. He was out in his own front yard in his
mackerel sloop. He was frozen right smack into his bay,
where my Aunt Elda could see where he was nights. And
couldn't do anything about it. But Aunt Elda could carry
a sack of flour out to him, or a pair of home-knit socks she
had run up, when he ran low and needed such things.

Yes, Winter had come, and the ocean had solidified around
my Uncle Thomas, but that did not keep my uncle from

[111]

being where he loved to be, at sea. He was always at sea on his farm. He was at sea when he should have been weaning his bull calves for veal, when he should be digging his potatoes, when he should be mowing the hay and hauling it in, and, to tell the truth, begetting another son to go with his single one. Still, knowing that sole son, I should say Uncle Thomas was a wise man not to tempt fate again.

Uncle Thomas ran away from the rural all the year, out to the Brown Cow or the White Bull for hake and pollock, out to the Grand Banks for cod. And when Winter sealed up his bay, he just ran a few hundred yards out over the bay ice and went aboard his sloop, got the fire up in his galley-stove, and settled down to whittling and teaching us boys, who also hot-footed it out over the bay ice right after him, when our mothers were looking the other way, how to grow up good sailing men, how to catch and clean and cure all kinds of Atlantic-Ocean fish, how to know the wind's ways and the weather's ways, and how to chew tobacco. Most of these arts our parents, who had visions of us all growing up to become bank presidents, runners of railroads, and masters of other easy ways of making a living, did not approve.

Of course, being locked in the bay like this, Uncle Thomas did not have much sea-room. But he made the most of what he had. If he was hemmed in horizontally and saw the same islands sawtoothed with the same fir trees out of the same port-holes all the time, my uncle wasn't hemmed in perpendicularly. There was the tide. He moved fourteen feet up

[112]

and fourteen feet down to his harbor's mud twice every solar day. It wasn't much, but it was something. Uncle Thomas made the most of what he had. When he was off the mud, he swore he felt his keel vibrate. He made us feel it, too. And he made allowances for the motion, just as if he were also moving on a horizontal plane. He knew what that sea motion was every minute of the time—how many minutes to high water, how many minutes to dead-low. He always cooked his victuals on the flood tide. And he washed the dishes—or rather let us boys wash them—on the ebb. Yes, Uncle Thomas kept tabs on the moon in her ancient mischief of bulging out the world's sides with salt water twice a day. He knew the old lady's curves every minute of the night.

And even if there weren't any waves to come at him and keep him alive, and even if his decks didn't tip up and keep him supple in the knees, at least being in touch with the ocean and moving up and down in his vessel, Uncle Thomas was free of women and his farm. His wife and his cows and his hens could not get at him out there in the snug boat that sailed and sailed but never got ahead of the farmhouse. Uncle Thomas had never trusted women, and he hated farms. They went together, in his mind. It was his wife who had tried to make a farmer out of him. She said Thomas was getting old, and ought to settle down to an easy life now, and make hay.

My uncle distrusted his wife's good faith, once he got tangled up in a borrowed mowing-machine. He had handled full-rigged ships, with a thousand lines and gadgets which had to be handled just so, but never, for sheer intricacy, had he ever run afoul of anything so complicated as a mowing-machine. He left cogs from the sorry thing all over his hay-field, until she finally broke down in the hay, and he left her with her teeth still stuck full of hay, for his neighbor to come and retrieve her and mend her if he could. And of course the neighbor couldn't. And Uncle Thomas had to pay for her out of his herring. Uncle Thomas had to do what little hay-ing he ever did afterwards by hand. He solved that problem by letting the cows right into the hayfield to cut their hay with their own teeth. When Winter came on, the cows were in the same boat with the grasshoppers that fiddled all Sum-mer and had to cry to the ants for their Winter supper. But, anyway, by Wintertime, Uncle Thomas' schedule of milking the cows only at dead-low tide, when the mackereling wasn't good, had got in its lethal work. Since the ebb tide shifted about so day to day, the cows got confused trying to keep abreast of it, and dried up altogether. So Uncle Thomas beefed the lot of them, and that settled his career as a dairy-man.

The hens, after devouring what scanty garden Uncle Thomas had, went over to the neighbors and dug up theirs. And they were knocked over and eaten by the irate neighbors for their pains, or they ran off into the woods and got eaten by the owls and the hawks. So that settled them. Uncle Thomas' farm problems were soon disposed of.

Taking to his sloop gave Uncle Thomas his chance to have

his revenge on the rural economy. He weaned the farms' sons
away from the land and did his level best to make good sailors
of them. He hoped to wean the sons away from women, too,
and so keep them from breeding sons who might return to
the soil, years to come. So all farms would peter out. As
small boys are naturally inclined away from the feminine
half of the world, my uncle found it all clear sailing with
us. He won us hook, line, and sinker.

Well, this red-letter year I speak of, Uncle Thomas invited
us boys, months before the ice shut him into up-and-down
sailing, to come out and spend Christmas with him. He didn't
have to invite us twice. We checked off the days with bated
breath.

When the Yule was actually upon us, some parents raised
objections. But short of tying their boys up, they could not
keep them from their fate. When our parents saw we were
bound to go aboard the sloop, they greased us over from
head to heels with goose grease against colds, put our heaviest
underwear upon us, and commended us all to God. They
gave us a last solemn warning as to what tobacco did to the
insides of little boys, and let us go. Most of us had a corncob
pipe or two, and all our fathers' tobacco we could stuff into
our brief breeches' pockets without giving ourselves away.
With a whoop we went aboard the *Elda J.*

The sloop was named after the wife of Uncle Thomas.
Uncle was willing to make that much concession to Aphro-
dite and the arts of home.

[115]

At the last moment, we boys decided not to let Uncle Thomas' own son come on board with us, though he had believed he was going to up to the last minute. We locked him up in the one-room annex to farm domesticity, and left him there, with the little building shaking with his fury. He was too big for his breeches when he was with his father, and his father could not teach him a thing. He cramped his father's style. He was best left ashore. So we set off over the ice, in a golden twilight, towards the little white heaven with one mast pointing to an early star. Cousin Frank was safely secured below hatches. Our cup was full. We went off into as complete happiness as ever little boys can know.

Uncle Thomas piped us aboard. At least, he stood with a wide grin showing under his gray moustache and counted heads. He had to return as many boys as came out, so he checked us off, and he gave us each a hand up the hawser at his bows, and a hand on the backside by way of greeting, when we got on deck. Uncle Thomas applauded and reprimanded us always with his big hand where we felt applause and reprimand the quickest.

Once on board, we were in another universe. Everything fell into a nautical schedule. As there were eight of us, we were told off into eight watches at once. There was to be no getting out of standing one's turn on deck when one's turn rolled around. Being the first one over the rail, I got the first watch of all. So I turned up my reefer collar and stayed right there on deck.

There wasn't a solitary thing moving in all that white uni-

verse with darkness coming on over it, around the frozen
sloop. But I kept my watch just the same. I paced back and
forth on the deck, to keep my toes from freezing. The stars
were coming out in the sapphire sky. It was so still I could
hear the sleigh-bells a mile away, over on Potts's Neck, as
belated fathers came home with presents to hang on the evening's tree. My breaths dogged me about. Uncle had a good
fire up, I could smell. For the sweet odor of dry spruce came
up the galley-pipe beside me. Every so often I put my red
mittens in the hot smoke and thawed out my hands. Every
so often the bay ice boomed, with a great crack going across
it. The tide was flooding. It got lonesome.

But the boat was alive under me. I heard tremendous
thumpings and runnings to and fro, down where I ached to
be. Uncle Thomas had steam up in the boys already, and
he was bellowing orders to them as they swept up the whole
cabin and put things all ship-shape and Bristol-fashion. Uncle
Thomas kept all hands alive.

A grog very much alive came up on the deck to me in the
hands of my Cousin John. It was mostly lemonade, but it had
a roof of nutmeg on top, and a good dash of rum below the
roof to keep the heat in it. I drank it down at one gulp. The
tears gushed out of my eyes and froze at once on my cheeks.
But I had fire burning in me that kept me hot to my hour's
end. The stars were all out over me and the sloop when the
next boy hove up on deck and replaced me. I went below
into the midst of Christmas.

I would never have known the cabin. Everything was

sanded white, and everything hung in its place. All I could see was boys' bottoms. All hands were on all fours around the grate of the galley-stove roasting beechnuts for Uncle Thomas' famous beechnut brittle. Captain Thomas—for that was what we had to call him the moment we were aboard—had shaved in our honor and in honor of the season. There was a sharp line along his high, weathered cheek bones where the razor had moved below the hairiness around his eyes which Captain Thomas never disturbed. He couldn't have shaved up 'longside his eyes, anyway; there were too many deep crinkles of laughter there.

Captain Thomas gave me his pan of thickening sugar-syrup to stir, to get the life back in my arms. One of the boys was eating too many of the roasted nuts, and Cap'n Thomas brought him to with a resounding slap on his curving stern where the underflannel was stretched its thinnest and let the tingling through best. After that, all the nuts went into the pan where they belonged.

There was no evergreen or holly. But Cap'n Thomas had got out several bottles of his red corals and hung them by the necks under the big snowy shells he had collected from all the islands of the Atlantic. And candles stuck up in his rum bottles had taken the place of kerosene lamps. The cabin smelled of beechnuts and Christmas.

The nuts were all done. The captain threw them into the soft candy. Then the vast hands of our skipper went into the sticky mess I was stirring, and his fingers worked the red-hot

triangular nuts we had gathered in October into the mess.
Uncle grabbed a fistful of the taffy and pulled it out like a
rope. He threw a loop of the stuff over my wrists, held on
to his own, and we started pulling away from each other for
dear life. Every so often, as things lengthened out, our skipper
threw another hank of the sweetness over still another boy
and ordered him to pull. We were all in it at last, bound
together in the little room below decks by a big rope of sweetness in which hot beechnuts crackled and sighed. When the
rope began to shred apart into brittle slivers, Cap'n Thomas
snatched it away from us and hung it up among the dark
beams overhead.

Captain Thomas got out the dough-dish and ran us up a
roomful of his notorious flapjacks. He sifted out a quart of
flour, whitening his best blue holiday pants all down the
front, threw in a tablespoon of salt, broke an egg into the
dish, poured in water and skimmed milk in equal amounts,
till the whole business was about like a pitcher full of white
lava. Then he bellowed for elbow room, told off one spry boy
to stay below on his knees and feed small spruce twigs into
the stove, got down his sideless spider, big as the wheel of a
baby-buggy, greased it with a great hunk of salt pork, and
poured out an island of the liquid flour on the hissing black
iron. Uncle Thomas had no truck with lady-sized flapjacks.
He made only man-sized ones—a whole spiderful at a time.
One spider, one flapjack. The island expanded and covered
the whole iron exactly to the edges, bubbles puffed up in it,

the edges crisped deep brown. Then Uncle Thomas, without moving so much as an eyelash, flipped the whole hot cake over true as a die. It leapt into the air, somersaulted, and came down right on the spider without overlapping anywhere on its circumference, and began browning on its other side. Not a muscle twitched in Uncle Thomas. I watched to see. But there the flapjack was, reversed. There was only a slight tremor at the tip ends of Uncle Thomas' moustaches. That was all. It was a miracle.

After every masterpiece of dough, Cap'n Thomas tried out slabs of fat salt pork till they were crackling dry chips. These he poured smoking on the big flapjack, slopped in a huge wave of maple syrup from a pitcher to hold the crispy pork sticks together, rolled the big flapjack up like a jelly-roll, spanked it down in the wood ashes sprinkled on the back of his stove, and went on to the next dough-devil.

The room filled up with blue smoke. You could cut the fog with a knife. We small boys coughed and got down on the floor to breathe the air coming under the door. But our eyes were shining like stars through that fog, with the light of hunger. Every so often Uncle Thomas leapt aloft and took a deep breath of the night and the stars in the sky, and came back stronger to his frying. The tier of flapjacks grew higher. Three flapjack-rolls to a boy. That was Uncle Thomas' rule. Three pounds to a boy.

The tier was completed at last. Uncle threw open the door wide and let the cold, pure night and the high starlight in.

[120]

"All right, boys. Fall to! These will put the whiskers on the bottom of your feet!"

We knew the whiskers were all a joke. But we fell to. We got outside those rolls of fried dough and salt pork and maple sugar in about thirty shakes of a new lamb's tail. As I recall them now, those Christmas flapjacks tasted like roast goose crossed with milk and honey and manna and quail. If I have whiskers today, on other parts of me besides my feet, I swear they started sprouting that holy night!

It *was* a holy night. Those flapjacks were only the beginning. While we were working the flapjacks down low enough inside us so we could sing, Uncle Thomas got out his backgammon board, his checker-board, and his chessmen, and we went to work. Uncle played the lot of us. He kept the whole three-ring circus of cocky little boys going, jumping a checker here, rooking his castle and king there, shaking double sixes out on the backgammon board. He beat the pants off the most of us, though I did win a game of checkers from him when he was singeing the ends of his moustache on a flaming match and his mind was turned inward. Captain Thomas doled the beechnut brittle out to us as we played. About a pound to a boy. That was the ceiling.

By this, our pipes were well open, and we sang. Not Christmas carols. Uncle Thomas had never lived much inside churches. But he had lived all over the seas and knew the songs sailors pull an anchor or turn a capstan by. He taught us the words—wonderful words of life!

Goodbye to Barcelona,
Goodbye to whisky neat,
There's a black-eyed girl a-singing,
The mangoes they are sweet.
Barcelona, Barcelon—aye—ay!
Whisky for the bosun,
A thousand miles away!

Then we all lit up our corncobs, and Uncle Thomas let himself right out straight into one of his best stories. The one about the time he was mate and ran afoul a whole gang of Havana black boys, who allowed they weren't going to load any sugar sacks into any man's hold on a Sunday, and he took a marlin spike to them and mellowed them down till they loaded that cargo in. Then he told the story of how the Maine captain who took his whole family south around the Horn one June had to get out his shears and make woolen pants for his molting hens to keep them from freezing to death.

One by one, what with the tales and the tobacco, the hot smoke from the galley-stove, and the sweet load of flapjacks in us, we boys fell over on the two bunks and slept where we lay, like so many logs.

But Cap'n Thomas did not sleep. He sat up and cut onions till the tears flowed from his eyes, sliced turnips, too, for the highwater mark of this Christmas, his wild-goose soup tomorrow. And as each boy's turn to stand watch came, he brought the boy to with a smack on the fuller sector of his

breeches, gave him a shot of the hot rum-lemonade, and sent
him on up aloft. Then Cap'n Thomas went back to his big
kettle on his stove. He had cut up salt pork and was trying
it out in the kettle's bottom. The good smell of it filled the
cabin. When the pork was good and brown, Uncle Thomas
poured in a jugful of water on it.

The wild geese Uncle Thomas himself had shot on the bay,
to be sure to get the plumpest ones, just before the ice made
in around him. He had hung the three of them for three
weeks from the sloop's mast, and ripened them off with
feathers still on them and entrails still in. They were ripe
now, and the feathers just fell from them. Uncle Thomas
took out the heart and liver and gizzard and threw them into
the salt-pork water in the kettle on the stove. He put in a
good dash of soda. Then he cut up the carcasses of the geese
and threw the pieces in. He let them cook for two hours,
till the meat was falling from the bones. Then he put in
his slices of turnip and onion. He let everything cook another half hour. Then he set the kettle on the back cover of
the stove, and in the narrow neck of early morning Uncle
Thomas ran up his little salt-dumplings. They were a secret
he carried to his grave. But I recall seeing him roll them out
under his gin bottle that holy night. He made what looked
like common piecrust and worked in a few large salt crystals.
He dropped each dumpling tenderly into the soup. He let
the fire run low, but the cooking went on all the rest of the
night, slow.

The sun slanted in on the relaxed boys on the bunks. One rubbed an eye, and his nostrils flared at the delectable odor. Another nose flared. Each boy wiggled his toes. He came to. His shoes were gone from him. He sat up in an aroma of heaven.

There below the bunk were our shoes, all right. And there was a bundle in them both. Uncle Thomas had his broad back-struts towards us, and his moustache was curved low over his kettle, twitching, as Uncle Thomas sampled the soup in a big spoon.

We fell on the bundles with whoops. And out of each roll of paper in the leather stockings Uncle Thomas had hung up for us as we slept, rolled an amazing little sloop or bark or brigantine, each exquisitely rigged with linen sails and shrouds of thin thread, each painted and polished for loving hours on end. They were the labor of a whole year, between mackerel and herring fishing. They were the work Uncle Thomas had busied himself with when he should have been hoeing potatoes and beans.

It was tip-top highwater mark under the good sloop *Elda J!*

"Merry Christmas, you lubbers!" Captain Thomas roared as he swung round on us.

It was wild-goose soup for breakfast, wild-goose soup for dinner, and wild-goose soup for supper all that blessed Christmas day. It tasted better each meal.

And each boy handled a small vessel which would be like the highwater mark of all the years of his life to come.

10. The Most Typical American I Know

HE ISN'T much to look at. He has lost some of his teeth and a good deal of his hair. His waist-line has got rather out of hand. He is too short for his weight. His hands are about the size of anchors, and they are crisscrossed with scars left by thousands of ropes and the thorny claws of lobsters. When he dresses up and puts on a white shirt, when a friend is married or buried, he looks like a weathered old house with a white picket fence around it. His skin is brown as an acorn or an Indian. He will never be able to get it white again. He has been out in fifty years of blue gales and fierce suns of the Maine coast. His face is a good map of all the weathers.

This man is a fisherman. He has dug twenty-five thousand bushels of clams, maybe, in his time, and taken a hundred thousand dangerous shears of live lobsters from his traps. He has poured out many tons of smelts and herring on his wharf, like streams of molten silver in the lantern light. He has fitted his love-life and his sleep-life in with the tides and seasons of the year. When herring have run heavy, love and sleep have had to take a back seat. He has worked every day since he was seven. He has taken a holiday twice, and he suffered agony both these two times.

Yet though he has lived over half his time on salt water, he is a farmer, too. He has raised his own eggs and potatoes and most of his meat. He is also a plumber, and a good one. He is a carpenter, and he built his own house. He is at times a stone-mason and an engineer. He has kept gasoline engines and motor cars going years beyond their normal life-span. He is a painter, a tinsmith, and a hunter. He is an amazing shot, and has brought down wild geese and coots in legions between his goings and comings as a fisherman-farmer.

This working man is also an expert in gunnery. He knows the science of ballistics. He knows the vitals of every gun from the catapults of the Romans to the eighteen-inch coast guns and "bazookas" of today. Keeping up with the history of artillery has kept him up with the history of man. He is well posted on that, too. Guns and men run pretty parallel. He knows more about the politics of ancient Babylon and mediaeval Byzantium than most college professors. He can refight our Civil War—in which his father took part—through all its least skirmishes up to Shiloh and Gettysburg's Little Round Top.

He doesn't stop with history. He can take any bone of the human body and name all the Latin promontories and capes upon it. He knows Gerrish's *Anatomy* by heart. But he also knows the *Bible*. In geography, he shines. He knows all the lesser capes and promontories there, too. Now when the sailing of ships is a lost art, like the architecture of the Cretans, he can name you every last line, every last curve on a ship, by their right names. He could step on a ship's deck tomorrow and sail her around Cape Horn. Ships, to be sure, are in his blood, for his ancestors lived on them all over the globe. He knows ships because the men who made his marrow learned exquisite lessons of wind and sea that were too fine to die out of their blood.

Though he fishes in a fourteen-foot boat, this man has men in his veins who sailed fourteen-hundred tonners. His ancestors are in Burke's oration on America. They helped build the United States by taking great whales off Antarctica and by carrying cargoes between all the continents.

This American is a story-teller, and he can take the smallest incident and make it into a breathless thing, full of the sparkle of humor and the salt of wisdom. Of course he can tell stories well, since he comes of a long line of story-tellers who kept hundreds of strong men from their work. This man keeps his hundreds from work, though he himself is working all the time he talks.

He is "up" on politics. He knows what is going on over the globe. He knows the time-servers and eye-servants and the demagogues who prey on democracy, and though they may sit in the seats of the mighty, he calls them fearlessly by name. He knows the honest men, for he is as honest as the lobster traps he makes. He has an idea of what America can be if we decide to go on the principle of the Golden Rule, at last, and sixteen ounces to the pound. He will make an able citizen in the coming United States of the World.

This man has not made much money in his life of hard work with his hands. But he has always been his own boss. He has never worked for so many hours a day, never kept one eye on the clock. He has worked for himself, and there is no cheating a boss like that. Many of his days have been fifteen-hour ones. He hasn't got rich, but he has sent his sons to college. He has earned his own house and many boats. He minds his own business, and he expects other men to mind theirs. He admires most the men who are free in their opinions, independent as he is, and willing to work as hard as he works. He admires men who get along. He likes men who want to get ahead in the world, improve their minds, and raise smart children like his own four boys. He is proud of his son's having been a soldier in the late war of liberation of people. He believes very much in common men, with fish-scales and earth on their hands, who fish and farm hard and believe hard in life and beget good sons and daughters to love life and live it well after they are done.

I think he is one of the wisest men I have ever come across. He works every day, but he never lives by the day. He lives far ahead in the future, where Americans have always been most at home—Emerson, Whitman, and the others. His wisdom does not come out of books, although he finds time to read books. It comes more out of his work, out of the weather and the land and the water, and out of his knowing and getting along well with working people.

This particular American happens to be a brother of mine. And I am proud to have so good a citizen in the family!

11. My Uncle Ancil

HE WAS only half an uncle. I never saw him in my life. He had gone out of Maine like a bright light long before I came into it. But the light of him lighted up all my boyhood. His blond hair and moustache shone from away off on the Pacific shore, over the width of a continent, and warmed me. He was my westering uncle. He was the American who refused to get over being a boy, who went west when our nation's boyhood went west, the American who rode off on horseback among the western stars. For me and my brothers this uncle was a myth. He was the Fountain of Youth. He was American history in the family pants.

This westering uncle still shines very near the top of the tree of my exuberant and unregimented uncles. Almost on the topmost twig.

Uncle Ancil was only my mother's half brother. But he had a grandfather of mine as his father, so he was in the family all right. He was one of the sons of my grandfather's first go at matrimony. Both my grandfathers, like so many American men of their time, had double crops of children. Ancil and his brother lived in the midst of a parcel of all girls in his father's second essay in wedlock. And he was the pivot on which the world rotated for my mother and her sisters. He kept their house like a band of bugles going, his step-mother in continual hot water, and his elderly stout-trousered father running like a boy as narrow as the wind, trying to keep up with him and undo the knots he had made of the family, the school, the church, the city, the county and—the Lord knows—maybe the Lord himself. Though he tried hard, my grandfather never did quite catch up with Ancil. He caught up just enough, now and then, to get his large hand home and hot on his back breeches. That was the only part he did catch up to. And hand, razor-strop, switches of birch or the looped end of a tug made no difference to Ancil. They only made him livelier.

No matter what mountains of mischief I got into as a boy, the best I could do was not halfway up to Ancil. My mother took great pride in pointing that fact out to me. If I rolled my father's ox-cart wheels out into the deep Atlantic, I heard how Ancil had beaten me by tipping both his father's upper and nether millstones in his grist mill into the river. How, his father never knew, but Ancil did it. When I tied two tomcats' tails together, I discovered that Ancil had been ahead of me and had tied four together and let the cats loose in the Baptists' Sunday night meeting. If I stuck a modest pin into the boy ahead of me in school where he bulged through the seat, Ancil, I learned, had rammed his step-mother's hatpin into Deacon Pillsbury, broadside to, as he knelt in Sunday meeting prayer. Ancil was always an inch, en ell, a mile or a continent ahead of my best. Yet he was a bright mark to shoot by. And I and my brothers shot. Hopefully.

The escapades of Ancil had become sagas by the time we all came along. There was the time he tipped the old German groceryman backward into his barrel of dill-pickles. In his struggles to get his portly self free, the German upset the barrel off his platform, rolled out of his store, bounced down High Street, down Middle, and split and came open on Front, and the brine poured into the river on its way to the sea. The barrel and the German both came open, they said. And people told about the time Ancil had climbed up the Congo belfry and filled the bell full of molasses, and he poised it somehow upside down there so that the ringer got a bath of the West Indies the first tug he gave to his rope.

Another time my Uncle Ancil put a sheet of fly-paper in Schoolmaster Merriman's chair. And the master had to ferrule Ancil with the chair still on his person. It was the high-water mark of the school year.

Ancil had the Old Boy in him, as his father put it, in the smell of onions. Unexpected mischief came out of small mischiefs he started. Ancil laid a powder train into the chest of fireworks in Wragg's Emporium on the night before the Fourth, and the whole city was lighted up not only by Roman candles and rockets nobody had to pay a red cent for but by Wragg's sofas and chairs. The Fire Department saved a few chairs and tables, and the walls of the store, but most everything else went up. Of course, Ancil was sorry about the furniture, and his father was sorrier still when he had to foot the bill.

Or take that time Ancil, who had by now grown up tall enough to think about washing behind his ears, set out to call on his girl. He borrowed a hand-car and tugged until he got it on the tracks. He set off under his own steam at a fine pace. And didn't the Seven O'Clock overtake him before he could get to his girl or get his car off the railroad tracks. The train hit the hand-car, that Ancil had left in a hurry, and nearly derailed itself. Ancil was a half mile away when the crash came, though the engine's headlight had been burning his neck when he started off. He had not intended to wreck the Seven O'Clock. It was only that he was in love and attracted lightning, as lovers do.

That was the secret of Ancil, I guess. He attracted the

powers of nature. Let that boy go to the seaside in his father's best buckboard, and thunder was sure to come up, the horse run away, and Ancil strew the family's vehicle and pieces of his father's heart all over the countryside. The lightning in Ancil's agile mind attracted the lightning in the sky. I once saw a turkey-cock, showing off to his hens, jump on a stump and gobble and bulge out big with his maleness right under a white thunderhead. And didn't the lightning fork right there in the clear sky ahead of the storm and spear that gobbler twice, and all that was left of his feathered maleness were two or three burning feathers? After I saw that happen, I understood the secret of Uncle Ancil. He was creative mischief. And when he started working, all the general mischief in the universe pounced right on him.

This lightning-attracter had been hard on my mother and the rest of the family, growing up. And then, when he was grown up, the boy was still in him big as ever. He was hard on them. But they all recalled him with great love. When he went out of their lives, to lighten up the west and seek his fortune, it was like a lamp being blown out. They all recalled that dark day. For this son who so constantly amazed an elderly father was as full of high spirits as a seven-year-old boy with his first dog. Every day that came along was a brand-new hound-pup to Ancil. He ran singing into the darkest days, and the days turned themselves inside out and came out all sunlight.

The night my grandfather's house burned down, for in-

Maine Farm

stance. My grandfather on mother's side got burned out fairly regularly. Fires seemed to follow in his wake, as did lively sons like Ancil. This was the first burning-out since he had acquired Ancil. There had been one or two houses burned before, and those had been sad occasions. But this one wasn't. Ancil was there. He turned it into a holiday. He played on his piccolo all through the fire and danced a hornpipe to it. Ancil's brains were in his heels, as his father put it, and he could dance the lively old dances like an angel. If angels *do* dance, and I believe they do.

There Ancil was, all through the vast shouting and carrying-out of commodes and horsehair sofas, the sound of falling timbers, his yellow curls running fire in the light that for once was at every window in a New England house. There he was playing rollicking tunes until even the firemen in their silver helmets and vast blue pants fell to dancing as they went and came smashing in windows with their hatchets and clanking with icicles on their gates-ajar moustaches.

Mother remembered that fire to her dying day. It had more to it than tragedy, though her best doll had been burned to cinders in it. It had a glory on it. It was Ancil. Six-year-old mother recalled how she sat in a Boston rocker on the hard-crusted snow, rocking her second-best doll with painted hair on her to sleep—the doll Ancil had climbed the ice-crusted verandah, after the firemen had forbidden him to go up the stairs in the house, to save for her. Mother rocked back and forth on the snow under the high sparks of her

home and the high stars to the tune of the *Arkansas Travel-
ler*. She was pure joy on runners.

The piccolo wasn't the only instrument my mother's half
brother could play. He could play a dozen. He could play
anything with notes on it or a hole to blow into. He had
mastered the accordion, the jew's harp, the violin, the cornet,
the piano, the flute, the oboe, drums, cymbals, the zither,
tambourine, and mouth-organ. He had almost mastered my
grandfather's bass-viol, but my grandfather discovered him,
and he played on Ancil with his bow till he broke it. Anything that had sound or rhythm in it was Ancil's meat. He
could even play *Annie Laurie* on his step-mother's best
water glasses filled to different levels with water. But he
reached his zenith on the harmonica. People used to say that
when Ancil had this pocket-organ cupped in his slim hands
and beat out the rhythm with his happy-go-lucky foot, he
brought out chords that made beefsteak-faced stablemen,
whom Ancil made his special friends, and little stable-boys
tougher than old nails, weep like so many babies. There was
hunger in those chords, and the tears of things.

Wherever hunger was, or great happiness, Ancil was right
there in the midst. He made the two of them seem much the
same. He liked best the things of faster or slower pitch than
the routines of life. They were life itself to him.

This uncle was, to hear them tell, a perpetual vacation.
Just to think of him kept my mother young and green up to
her grave. Ancil had come into a New England family, into

[140]

a time and a community where paying attention to business was a life-long business from short skirts to the shroud. It was the law of life. And Ancil was a vacation from it. He never paid attention to any business, save music and fun. In a land of long and hard Winters he was a perpetual Spring. No wonder the little boys and the big loved him and followed him.

Uncle Ancil must have been the finest big boy for a small boy to worship there ever was. It is a deep sorrow of my life that I did not have him around to grow up to in the flesh. I had to do it *in absentia*. This Ancil knew all the best holes for trout and brought them home, without a line, tickled from under their stumps by his bare hands. He was a dead-shot with anything from a sling-shot to his father's eight-gauge shotgun, and he came home from Merrymeeting Bay weighted down with wild geese that weighed more than he weighed. If he could have sawed wood as he could bring down squirrels, my grandfather used to say, Ance would have made a fortune already while still in his teens. But squirrel pies are good things as well as fortunes. And there are too many Jacobs in this world to steal the birthright, and the very breeches, off the hairy hunters, the Esaus and Ancils of this world. There should be laws to protect the boys of us, from Dan'l Boone to Kit Carson, who have kept us in skins and opened up a continent to civilization.

Uncle Ance opened things up all right, in the traditional American ways and in new ones of his invention. While he was mastering the piccolo and the deer-rifle, and playing hooky from school, Ancil so discouraged my grandfather that he gave up trying to civilize him and put him into a Bath shipyard building ships. So the youth had a hand in one or two vessels that went out from his little Kennebec city and carried the world's goods around the world.

But ships were not Ancil's trade. They were too slow for him and his quick ways, too big for him to handle all by himself. He had to take orders from a boss. That was one thing Ancil would not knuckle down to. So he gave his piccolo away. His zither and his cornet. But not his mouth-organ. That fitted into his pocket easily. Ancil gave away what was left of his violin, and followed Horace Greeley's advice and went west to open up America. So I lost a golden chance to get acquainted, before it drifted west, with an essential America, to grow up with and grow wise with a belated Dan'l Boone.

They said, mother used to say, that Ancil left the shipyard very fast, just ahead of his boss, into whose voluminous trousers he had just dropped a white-hot bolt he had in his tongs. The man's trousers gaped continuously behind, and Ancil never could resist gaping trousers. So Maine lost a promising pioneer early.

The folks heard from Ancil every other year or so. Or other people sent home word for him. He was covering the country all right. He had wet his pants in the Mississippi, been in a Kansas cyclone and an Arkansas cloudburst. He

had been robbed twice, and shot at several times, but they
had missed him. He was getting along fine. Ancil was using
his young wit, that was sharp as a razor, trading in the Dakotas. He had made a bee-line for the Indians. He had always
fancied Indians. Being, as his old father often swore, a Red
Indian himself, Ancil made quick friends with the Indians.
He wrote home that he had been adopted into one or two of
their tribes. But going Indian did not take permanently.
That would have meant settling down and staying put, two
things Ancil was constitutionally unfit to do. But he learned
from the Sioux and Dakotas to be a great hunter of buffalo.
He sent his mother home a buffalo hide for her parlor from
St. Joe. He sent his father a pair of buffalo horns. Ancil had
let his hair grow. He had tried to let it grow as a boy and
had drunk a gallon of hard cider once on the quarter dollar
his sire had given him to have his curls shorn. He had mastered the fiddle under that stimulus. His father had caught
him and cut his hair with the horse-clippers that time. Now
Ancil let his curls grow as they would. They were down on
his shoulders. With all that spun-gold on his head my mother
used to talk about he must have looked like a sunrise on the
prairies.

My westering uncle wrote home about waking up in a
pond of prairie dew and eating a bison's tongue grilled on a
stick over his camp-fire coals for breakfast. He wrote home
of casing his body in creek clay and robbing bee-trees full to
their bark with barrels of honey. He wrote of knocking down

ten prairie chickens with one bullet. Game was plentiful. He was living off the country and growing happy as a porpoise.

But Ancil wrote back, too, of seeing a prairie fire coming down on him like a yellow continent, and of his back-firing the prairie grass, taller than his tall curls, before it reached him and cooked him like the buffalo steaks he ate from that morning after the fire. Another time, he was almost cooked on his shady side as he lay with his mouth in a runnel of water as the fire went over him. His seat smoked, he wrote home, for hours. Any boy alive would have given his right hand to be out there with Ancil. He would have given his best glass-alley to be with Ancil, smoking seat and all, and doing what he was doing every day.

My uncle stood up to a cyclone of a thousand buffalo thundering and coming black and shaggy, with their little red eyes burning with madness and terror deep in their lion-like heads like lightning, ahead of a wall of flames coming on the wind like the wind and devouring all the world. My uncle stood up with his two revolvers smoking and cut him a swath without moving an inch through the heart of the herd. A boy would have given his best kite, and his Barlow knife to boot, to do such a thing.

My westward uncle was living by the skin of his teeth and the quickness of his eye trained from babyhood to see the bright promise of joy ahead. He was up to his eyes in bison and Indians and adventure such as most boys can only dream about with an ache in them. Uncle Ancil was breaking wild horses, he was riding prairie ponies like the wind before the wind. He was going on, going west, getting younger and handsomer as the years went by. And sober relatives, I and the others, in Maine, were staying home, minding our dull business, doing what little mischief we could, and getting soberer and duller year by year. It was a tragedy!

Wherever life hung by a thin bright hair, or men lived quick and fast, my Uncle Ancil was hanging by his shining curls and living fast and handsome. My grandfather before he died, I am sure now, must have wept tears for this Absalom, the fair-haired son who might have kept the sunlight on his late afternoon of life, he had lost to the young America going west.

This uncle who had grown a myth was thistledown and forked lightning on the horizon of the world far to the west. Beloved of the Red Men, friend of the prairie dew and the quail, Uncle Ancil was flourishing while I was getting ready to be born, getting my first teeth in Maine, getting into my first forked clothes, and missing the chance of a lifetime to stay young and stay American forever.

Uncle Ance took his sweet time going west, going into history. He was in no hurry. History could wait and grow up with him. He wanted to take time to see and be America. He was seeing and being it. Living off its fat lands and lean, drinking out of its rivers, wrapping its starry nights around him like a cloak, making his bed of its valleys. He was reliving America's childhood and manhood. He was leaning his body down to withing in sharp winds and toughening his bones and muscles in frosts and storms. And I was learning my *ABC's* off the Wood-Bishop, Bangor cookstove in a tame Maine kitchen!

This uncle of mine wrote home to my mother, years after it happened, how he had been in the Bad Lands of the Black Hills when a nation of angry Sioux fell on the long-curled Custer and shot him and his stout blue men into ribbons in the last tumultuous victory the Indians were ever to have. Uncle Ancil was so near the Little Big-Horn that he could smell the smoke of carbines on the wind, hear the bugles and the blood-curdling yells as tomahawks and sabres cut heads in halves to their chins. He said, jokingly, that he did not go over personally to stop the trouble because his portmanteau was checked for a depot farther west. And, anyway, Uncle Ancil liked Indians and did not want to spoil their day's sport. He was betting on Sitting Bull and his other Sioux friends.

All the same, friends or no friends, my Uncle Ancil wrote that he took care that night to sleep with his horse tethered to his right ankle through the flap of his tent. He did not show a light but ate in the dark. And through his dreams he heard the thundering Sioux shaking the earth with their ponies. The thunder and warwhoops got so close at last that Uncle Ancil woke up, and he pulled his whinnying horse right into his tent and muzzled him tight with his hands on his throat till the warwhoops faded out into the night. So

Ancil had his hair, as he wrote home—his curls his mother used to do up on her fingers—still on his head in the morning. To his red friends all blond hair looked alike. So, once more, he stood on the edge of American history and heard it happening.

West and west Ancil went, and all that boys love best went with him. He crossed the lands of the Mormons, and had good praise for them out of the *Book of Genesis* for having more than one slender string to their matrimonial bows. The multiplied wives sort of appealed to him. He would have liked to stop and take two or three wives himself and get religion, but, as he put it to my mother, he and religion never had mixed. So he rode on west.

My Uncle Ancil saw the alkali rivers ringed with white death and the hollow eyes of skulls. He passed through the ribs of the world, through its dry skeleton, over mountains like those dead ones on the moon. He climbed the High Sierras at last, and went down by the road over that incredible turquoise set deep in the world where the Donner party ate one another and died under the sixteen-foot drifts of Winter. He saw the high firs pointing up towards him, frosted with unbelievable light, a mile down under his horse's hoof, as he rode along the shelf where a misstep meant death in a deep valley full of rainbows. He came down steeply into golden California. He saw the sequoias older than Christianity holding up the young sky above the canyons. He saw the miners, bearded and gimlet-eyed, their pants bulged with knives and death, wading the steep rivers and washing the sand for the golden pay-dirt. He swopped stories and coarse jibes with them. He ate their gray dough and evilly-old meat. But Uncle Ancil did not stay with the miners. He wasn't after nuggets. He was after life, after perennial boyhood, after having a good time as he had been since he first leaped out of his cradle and astounded his heavy-built father by turning into a light being with wings on his heels.

My uncle went on to the Pacific. He wet his winged feet in that. He built him a house of California cedar. He lived off the deer and the quail. He lived high and was happy, he grew prosperous, but not like his father back home; there was always a leanness in his make-up. People heard he had got him a wife at last, got him a ranch, and got himself several sons. Every once in a while, my mother had word of him. Faint, but still a word. It seemed he had got himself a fortune after all. His cattle and his sons swarmed over California. But for all his fortune Ancil had not lost his boyish laugh or his sense of fun. He was still a small boy with his first hound-pup.

The sound of Uncle Ancil faded out as the years came faster along. Mother heard of him only every second year. Then only every third. But all was well. He was happy. He was even younger.

By the time I came along and had my first hound-pup, Uncle Ancil had gone out into silence. He had faded into a legend. He was like a lively tune out of an earlier day. My mother sang the song to me. It was a lovely one. I never tired of hearing her sing it. It was the song of the way the older Americans took on their young way to make a nation. It was a song of strong men who refused to get over being boys, of men who went back ten thousand years to the youth of our race, to the running deer and the starry roof overhead, a song of hunger, a song of men living lonely by their muscles and wits as brothers to sunrise and sunset.

Hearing that old song, I was sure that my Uncle Ancil's hair was still on his shoulders, without a gray hair among the golden, like the curls on my own head that my mother twisted up each morning on her fingers. I knew he was still lighting life up somewhere, out there in romantic space, on a different ocean from mine. The world was all right still. And Uncle Ancil would always be there somewhere, shining.

And my Uncle Ancil still is. He has escaped time, devourer of all things. He is the man who never got over being a boy. He is American history. I am proud I have American history for an uncle.

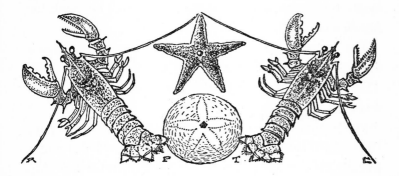

12. My Other Unforgettable Character

SOME time ago, I wrote about my father, as an unforgettable character. He was an unforgettable character all
right, an all-round American man who did many things well.
One of the pleasantest responses I had to that piece, when it
came out in a magazine, were some letters—mainly from
women—and the burden of their song was this: If your father
was such a saga-sort of man, what on earth must your mother
have been? She must have been a wizard or an angel!

My mother was. She was both, in just the proper proportion. She had to be, to keep up with such a man as my father and raise the ten of us children in such out-of-the-way places as we grew up in.

Now my father, though he wore a stand-up dickey and striped pants on Sundays, had the old pioneer in him bigger, as mother used to say, than a woodchuck. He was not at home unless he was breaking in new steers, new islands, or new boys and adding them on to civilization. Though he owned houses in town and carried on several businesses there, he did not trust modern improvements too much. His bank was an earthen pot he kept in a stonewall. He went Dan'l Boone the minute he got out of his town buckboard and town pants. He ran for his axe, his patched pants, and his oxen and dory.

So my mother had to do housekeeping in hard places and learn to piecen out our food, medicines, and games from wild woods and the sea. She made us puddings from the seamoss we gathered from the reefs at ebb tide; she gathered hemlock bark, pennyroyal, and yarrow to keep our medicine closet stocked against illness. She doctored us with wild flowers and herbs, for few doctors could get to us over the wild ocean in months like March or December. We children gathered her wild honey from dead trees, and apples the old Indians had sown went into her jellies and tarts to put iron and flavor into our bones.

That mother of mine introduced tame strawberries and

apples into clearings she and we boys hacked out of the balsam thickets. But she also lived off the wild. She put up wild raspberries, gooseberries, currants, huckleberries, and blueberries. Her cellar was like a cathedral with stained glass of hundreds of jars of jams and preserves letting the light through. But there were lobsters and crabs and mackerel in jars down there, too. Mother kept enough canned things ahead to last ten years. That was her margin of safety. In every season, her preserve-kettle was simmering on the back of the stove and filling the whole house with scents of forest or sea.

Just the other day I ate some wild crabapple-jelly, and those crabapples grew on our saltwater farm over fifty years ago, before I was born or "thought of!"

We children sometimes gathered cranberries on the salt-marsh by lantern light when frost in the air threatened our Winter's sauce for roast-goose. We fought the red squirrels for every beechnut and hazel-nut on the farm; we took the blackberries just at their heaviest right from under the sharp noses of the raccoons. When smelts were running in September, the little boys of the family wallowed up to their eyes by lantern light in silver continents of fish, picking out the baby bluefish and herring which mother would "lay down" in stone crocks with vinegar.

Always we had to pay our tithe to the simmering preserve-kettle out of the hundreds of crates of huckleberries we picked in August to buy our year's shoes and stockings with. Mother took her toll of the eels and flounders we speared, the lobsters and crabs we took from our homemade traps.

Mother was the warden of the cellar, and she kept a solid foundation of food under us. I think we could have lived fat for a whole year without ever moving out of our house if the weather had decided to be all storms and had cut us off completely from the rest of the world. Mother could have beaten bad weather for a year.

It was the same with wood for the stove. Each boy had his "stent" of so many armfuls to saw up and lug in as his share of the family's prosperity, just as every girl had so many seams to sew or so many rooms to sweep a day. But, by the same token, Mother would lend a hand bending the bows of a boy's first lobster trap and cut out dresses for a girl's doll. She helped us as much as we helped her. She was a wizard. at laying the ribs for a boy's dory. She steamed the oak in her own teakettle to make it curve the right way.

Our family always lived a long ways from markets and schools, doctors and neighbors. We learned to do for ourselves. Sooner or later, mother used to say, she had lived on every jumping-off place among the many islands of Casco Bay. Casco was full of untamed islands. Father always chose the wildest he could find. He didn't have to live out there. He had houses in town. But he loved to live there. For he had a family of boys he wanted to train to be good hunters and fishermen, carpenters and boat-builders and masons. He knew wild islands were the places to bring up boys right. So my father tamed one savage island after another to human use.

Let me call the roll. There was Spruce. That was before I came along. My father was the only man on that island almost the bigness of a township. But he filled it. Mother had to fight the hawks to keep them from carrying off her full-grown Plymouth Rocks. It was so wild on Spruce the eagles carried off our lambs; and once when mother set a lantern on the headland one wild November night, to light my father into the little harbor there, a bald eagle flew down, seized the lantern by its bail, and took it away over the spruces, scattering light far and wide as he went off to sea.

It was like living right in the middle of an epic poem, all right.

Winters, my father had to drive his yoke of oxen over a good part of the frozen ocean to come home there. One night his oxen went through, and he stood there alone and stared sorrowfully into the black water where his fortune had been swallowed from sight. Another Winter night father went through himself; but mother, always a light sleeper as becomes a pioneer mother, heard him cry out. She got up and slipped on a coat, ran down to the bay and out on the ice with a pole and a lantern, reached out her pole and drew father out of the death he was in up to his armpits. And the fire forever burning on her hearth warmed him back to life.

Nights of loneliness and fear there were many, but my mother faced them and came off with flying banners. She raised babies by bold water, where a misstep meant sudden death and one less child. She might nurse a baby at the bean-patch's end and then go back to her hoeing. It was all in the day's work. She taught my brothers to spell between wheel-barrows of rockweed she was hauling up to fertilize her roses with. For she turned fir forests to roses as well as curly-headed babies. Mother rowed her small children home from raspberrying on neighboring islands, with one sawed-off sailor in very short pants lending her a hand on an oar two times his length. She rowed the children home through fogs and snow-squalls. But she always brought them home safe. Her children grew up very much at home in woods where bobcats howled, among dories and bell-buoys, lighthouses and high rolling waves.

One lonesome stormy night mother was hulling her November corn, and she became aware of a face staring in on her through the window in the dead of the night. She swung round. It was an evil-looking face, and its nose was flattened to the wet pane. It was an Indian. Mother sat petrified. She heard him come round to the door, lift the latch, and come in. He said not a word to her. He undid his bundle of birch baskets and set them out to dry on the hearthstones before the fire. He left them and vanished again into the night. Next morning, at crack of day, the Indian came back for his baskets. He counted them. He grunted his thanks. Then, by sign language, he ordered my mother to fetch him a piece of cloth. He swept it up full of ashes from the hearth, knotted it into a bag, and threw it into mother's big kettle of hulled corn. It was what his squaws had always done. It was the Indian touch. The wood ashes peeled off the skins from the swollen kernels of corn as no lye ever had done it so well. So mother learned one more trick from the wild, to pay for harboring the Indian's baskets.

Another time of storm, with father away as so often, in broad daylight, mother saw a schooner go over hard by her island, heard the men of its crew singing out for help as they struggled in the water. Mother launched the dory from high-water mark to the tide's way, and pushed off to save them. But the waves ran so high she could make not an inch of headway against them. She tugged at the oars in vain and heard the cries go out one by one as the men drowned. It was a scar on her mind always.

The next island was Pond Island. We lived on that. It was out even nearer to Spain than Spruce. I cut my teeth on its granite ledges. I learned the alphabet there, with gulls screaming past like squalls of snow, and the nearest neighbor two miles of open ocean away. Our house had to be anchored down with hawsers when the gales came and beat on it. My mother shifted the ropes when the wind changed, if father wasn't there at home to do it. She made the kitchen window into a lighthouse every night, setting the lamp there to guide him home from his lobstering far at sea. It was a lonesome place, except for us. We were too many and too busy to mind the vast solitude around us. But our cow minded it. She would go to the landward end of the island and low towards the four-footed friends she had left on the main. She finally got nervous prostration and dried up completely for loneliness.

We lived snug on Pond, in spite of the winds that went over forever. Mother kept us warm with driftwood the waves brought in from far places. She taught us all, boys and girls alike, how to rig lines and catch the cod at our front-doorstep. She kept the kettle boiling, and we could land our fish and almost throw them into the kettle for dinner. We could not go to school, of course, so mother became our school teacher, and she made us toe the mark with decorum just as if we were at school and start off on the nose of nine o'clock and keep our noses to our books till noon. She taught me, the youngest, to add, subtract, and multiply by the white seashells I brought up from the beach.

When we moved away from there, my father took us, house and all, in his schooner, up the bay a bit closer to civilization, and set us all down on another wild island.

That was Sebascodegan. There our wandering house was finally anchored for good, and I grew up the rest of my height there. It was a wild place I lived in, still. We children helped clear the forest and build our house bigger, build a barn, and fences, both land and water ones, to keep our cows home. Mother pitched in, when we were short-handed, and helped with the haying and the turnip-pulling. She took over all our cabbages and onions and lettuce, beets, and kidney beans. She wouldn't trust us with the "garden sass." She had a way with asparagus and strawberries, currants and gooseberries. They were her province. She weeded them by hand. She helped father with his twenty hives of bees. She had a way with bees, too. She could handle them where father got stung so he had to run into the ocean and shed his trousers. Mother had complete charge of the hundred hens. The eggs were her pin-money, and she used her pin-money to have little extras, like piano lessons or a very special doll for a girl that had not skipped sweeping her room for a whole year. She never let one of us come near her hens. She whitewashed the henhouse and cleaned it out all by herself. Children put hens out of their serenity, she always said—especially boys. But she did let us boys crack up crabs she had cooked to make her Plymouth Rocks lay better.

When we were small, mother did most of the milking, night and morning. She had to, for father kept ungodly hours, going and coming as he did, and the cows would have dried up if she had left the milking to him. She taught each of us boys how to milk, as soon as our fingers got long enough to reach around the teats, and so she got time to put in a new patch of raspberries in her kitchen garden.

Mother made most of our clothes. The boys' were easy. For she just cut down father's coats and pants to our sizes. Being the fourth boy, I got my father's trousers at four removes, and wearing rather thin, but I was proud to have even that much of my magnificent sire! The girls were another matter. Mother had to use her artistry there. For them, with her sewing-machine, mother turned out as lovely "tires" and dresses as any of the smartest girls in town flaunted. She was especially good at embroidery and laces and ruffles. Girls wore a lot of those then. What was more, mother taught every last girl as she grew up to turn out dresses for herself as good as she could make.

Of course the cooking fell to mother also, though my father lent an expert hand when a cod's-head chowder was on the ways. With her vast pioneer kettles, old-fashioned earthen crocks and iron spoons, and a fireplace always going full blast, as well as the kitchen stove, in the six cold months, mother turned out square rods of roast meats and roast fish, baked, boiled, and jugged. How many acres of golden johnnycake and gingerbread she made for hungry boys no one but an astronomer could figure out. She could run up a cake to make the heart sing out of almost nothing but a few blueberries. She was the best cook I have ever known.

My mother had to do without a good deal in the way of boughten things; she made out with imagination and home herbs and spices, with the clams and lobsters from the bay, home-grown pig, with venison, wild geese and wild ducks as well as the tame ones we raised on the farm. She made out very well. She knew all the tricks of the solid old pioneer housekeeping; she kept her milk sweet in a dark cupboard, till the cream rose on it like a piece of yellow velvet half an inch thick; she put the butter down the well to keep

it hard and savory; she put her fish in vinegar for the Winter, in crisscross layers, and they came out of the vinegar
and cloves without bones. Without refrigerators, miles and
months from ice, she kept her meats unspoiled and tasty.
She was a wizard with smoke and salt. She defied the heat
and came off triumphant.

Well, you might think that a woman with her heart and
hands and head so full with cooking, sewing, and cleaning
for ten children, and keeping a house ship-shape in a wilderness surrounded by the sea, would have little time for culture
or refinement; you might get to thinking of a big raw-boned
peasant-sort of woman. Mother was small and delicate, a
quiet little woman, and gentle as the west wind. I never
heard her raise her voice to correct a rough boy on the rampage in my whole life. But that gentle word of hers was law.
She was like the Rock of Gibraltar when she made up her
mind; nothing could move her. She had a will like a New
England swamp maple. Her wit, too, was like a razor, and
her judgment infallible. I never knew her equal for sizing a
person up accurately. She knew when a man or a boy was
"small potatoes and few to the hill." But, best of all, when
she knew he was small, she kept it to herself and never hurt
his feelings by letting him know that she knew.

I have never known a woman who wore her fine clothes
better than my mother. When she came out of the henhouse
and dressed for company, she blossomed out into a very ele-

gant lady indeed. And she held her own in polite conversation after she had done a big washing and ironing. She had fine manners. She could talk about books and what was going on in the world with the best-read people. How she found time to read books and keep posted on affairs, goodness only knows, but she found it.

My mother was an angel all right, as well as a centurion—a seraph in fact, for she was an angel with granite and iron in her spine, and she got what she wanted done.

When father died, mother took over the whole family, moved us to town, saw her children through school and several through college. She kept the Sebascodegan farm still, as her anchor to windward, to keep us in milk and eggs and hard work with our hands and backs, for the good of our souls. With us to help, she kept the farm going as well as her big town house. She went every Sunday to church, in her Sunday best, and she took us all with her. Only something of the calibre of pneumonia could excuse us.

One of us children became an invalid. Mother took full care of him and did everything for him for fifteen years. But you would never know there was a shadow in her house.

This strong small woman was the center of her sons' and daughters' lives for forty years, even when they began to have hordes of children of their own. She was like the head of a clan, and grown men and women consulted her as they had done when they were in short pants and short dresses.

She sat in the midst of twenty-eight grandchildren at the last. She laid down the law even to them. Like Cornelia, she could say: "These are my jewels."

My mother was a model American mother, a pattern the world would do well not to lose. A hard-worker, yet a thinker and a planner, too. A believer in the family, a believer in large families, willing to live her best life in her children, a woman of foresight, and thrift, yet vision, she did her part to train a fair segment of America to be independent and thorough and hard-working and yet trust most to the spirit and sound character. She wanted her children to get ahead in life, rise higher than their parents, be better men and women, or fine carpenters and teachers and poets maybe, but fine parents in any and every case.

And I like to think it was my mother's pioneering with father, matching her will against the wind and weather, making out by her own wits and energy, on out-of-the-way islands, that made my mother the builder of men and women she was.

This mother always had the management of all our flowers. Her flower-garden was always the show-piece of whatever island she lived on. She had dories full of petunias; her lilacs and rosebushes filled the dooryards full. The morning-glories that ran up the twine strings by the back-doorstep were always her doing. I think of her still whenever I smell sweet-peas. For they were a special achievement of hers.

On our last farm of all, among wild popples and bayberry,

there are three lovely circles of fierce, tame light burning white every May that comes back green to the world. The wild things have tried their best to choke out those tame circles of white, but they have not been able to kill them. They are the narcissus my mother had as the center of her flower-bed. The other flowers are gone now, but these, untended, stay on. The woman who planted them has gone to sleep in the earth, but her flowers keep her name shining and alive. Strong and fragrant as ever, there could never be a whiter or better monument to an unforgettable woman.

Yes, seraph is the word—white and fragrant and full of life.

III

MAINE INDIVIDUALISTS
ON THE LOOSE

13. Uncle Henry

HE WASN'T really an uncle to anybody. But every boy in the village wished Uncle Henry *was* his uncle, and every boy wanted to grow up and live just like him. For Uncle Henry never took orders from any man, never had a steady job, and never wanted one. He lived off the blueberries. He lived off the rabbits. He lived off the flounders in the bay. When he had to have a meal of victuals, he went fishing, or he went hunting. He did everything for fun. Between times, he just whittled and followed the sun around his shack in the clearing in Trufant's Woods.

Hard-working fathers, jawing their sons for going off fishing instead of sawing up the Saturday stent of cord-wood, would say, "You are going to grow up another Uncle Henry, that's what you're going to do!"

The boys only wished they could.

People said it was a shame for a man to live on wind-pudding and waste his whole life the way Uncle Henry did. A man should have some gumption to him, grow up and amount to something. Look at Mr. Black. He started from nothing, and now he owned three sawmills. Look at Dave Peabody. He went to fight the Germans, and he captured a whole platoon of them and lost his leg and came home a hero. But no one could expect a thing of Uncle Henry. He just sat. He was an awful example to the young. He was no more use than a last year's crow's nest. That was what people said.

And a lively loud whistle came down the road, and behind it came Uncle Henry, slouching along with patches as big as barn-doors on his seat, and his fishpole over his ragged shoulder. And behind Uncle Henry came his hound-dog Cyrus, lean and happy-go-lucky as his master, without a thought in his head but off for a lazy good time.

Henry said his dog was a powerful smart dog for rabbits. The boys said so, too. But grownups said the dog was a chronic loafer, a sheep-thief, with no license to his name, and the dog-catcher ought to collar him and put him out of the way. Like master, like dog.

But Cyrus slumped along after Uncle Henry with his eyes running over with love and admiration. Happy-go-lucky pair! They never knew what trouble was. Trouble kept away from their tumble-down door.

It was that last week of the worst drought for sixty years when trouble came to Trufant's Woods. The slash that Mr. Black's portable sawmill had left last August caught afire, nobody knew how. Before anyone could lift a hand, the flames had run through the dry boughs like tinder and were climbing up the tallest pines in the woods. The tall trees shivered, smoked, then burst like rockets into sheets of fire. Everybody in the village got his shovel out. The fire-engine drove out. But no one could get within three rods of those exploding trees. A man couldn't keep his face towards the flames but had to look sidewise. It was a tornado of a fire. The flames walked right through the heart of the forest. The ground shook with earthquakes of the falling pines. The men just leaned on their shovels, looked at the fire sidewise, and let her sing.

Uncle Henry came running with his fishpole trailing and the patches on his seat flapping open like wings. He burst into the group of watchers. He had run all the way from the bay. He could hardly get a word out, he was so out of breath.

"My house! my house! Will—will it catch my house?"

It was the first anybody had thought of Uncle Henry or his house. The men caught sight of the house now, where the trees had been burned in front. It was still there. But the tall flames were walking in on it from three sides.

"Your house will go like popcorn, Uncle Henry, in another minute!" the men sang out. Then they laughed. "Yes, sir! She's a goner!"

"I've got to get in there."

Uncle Henry put his head down and ran straight at the crackling brush.

"Hey! you half-wit! You can't do anything to save her. You'll be burned alive. Come back!"

But Uncle Henry wasn't coming back. He stumbled in the embers and got up all sparks, but he kept right on.

"Grab him, somebody!"

Two men more daring than the rest ran in and grabbed the man by the arms. But there was no holding Uncle Henry. He fought, he bit them in the arms. He was like a wild man. He got away. He screamed out something, and ran on.

"It's that dog of his. He's in there. He left him to home."

The two men rubbed the bitten places in their arms. No one could do a thing. They all stood there with their mouths wide open and watched.

They saw the man reach the door. It wouldn't open. He threw himself against it. It gave, and Uncle Henry went in. Just that instant three blazing pines leaned over and came down. Where the shack had been there was only a mountain of wicked fire.

The men found Uncle Henry's bones when things cooled down. They were white as chalk. It was easy to make them out. And all mixed in with them were the smaller bones of the hound. When the men touched them, the bones fell all together into fine dust. They did not try to separate what was left. They scooped up all the white dust together and put it in a box. They took the box to the graveyard. And they buried it right next to the big, fine monument on the Black family lot.

It wasn't a regular funeral. But all the men were there, and they all took off their hats when the box was lowered into the grave. All the men's Adam's-apples worked up and down, and no one felt like saying anything about happy-go-lucky loafers ever again.

All the boys were there, too. They knew they had lost the best uncle they would ever have. They looked it. You could tell it by their proud and shining eyes.

14. The House Divided

IT STARTED as a molehill. But before long that molehill grew up into a good-sized mountain, and there was a house cut clean in two, with the husband on one side and the wife on the other.

It started over Sam's saying that Lucy's Great-Aunt Sarah had an eye like an adder.

Now Lucy had said so herself, to begin with. But that was

just after Aunt Sarah's will had been read and Lucy had found out that Aunt Sarah had left her only a pair of jet earrings, and not a red cent of money. Time had mellowed that aunt, though. And, anyway, a person in the family could say things about a relation an outsider could not.

Lucy had got awfully angry when Sam got short with her that day and said a pound of common crackers was all any woman could use, and two was foolish extravagance, and then he up and twitted her on her Aunt Sarah's eyes. That was the last straw. Lucy got good and mad.

When Sam's wife got mad, she stopped talking. She stopped now. She stopped for a whole fortnight. It was the longest she had ever stopped. It had been for just a day or two up till then. Sam talked to her, but Lucy did not talk to him. Sam tried every way to get her to speak back.

It was only when he came in from town and told her he had got only eighteen cents a dozen for her eggs that Sam got a word out of Lucy.

"Cat's hind foot!" shouted his wife. "That's highway robbery!"

Sam grinned in triumph. The ice was broken at last. But Sam couldn't leave a good thing alone.

"They was only pullets' eggs," said he. He should have known better.

That was when the last words were said and the long silence began, the silence that became a town landmark.

"Sam Lawson! From now on you and me are strangers.

You keep your ideas to yourself, and I'll do the same. You keep to your half of the house, and I'll keep to mine."

And Lucy went to work. She got her a piece of chalk. Sam stood there with his eyes bugged. His wife drew a line from the middle of the kitchen door-sill, under the middle of the cookstove, right across the kitchen, under the kitchen table, through the bedroom door and under the bed. The stove was halved. The table was halved. The bed was halved. The whole house was. Lucy had the cooking side of the stove, the sink, the dishes. Sam had the woodbox. All his coats hung on her side Lucy flung over on Sam's. She moved her bureau and her clothes to her side of the bedroom.

Sam got his back up. He would bite his tongue off before he would say a word that wasn't wanted. He was a stubborn man. If that was the way Lucy wanted it, it was the way he wanted it, too.

It went on so for months, for years. The woman cooked the victuals and pushed them to the middle of the table. Sam ate them and pushed the dirty plates back. Lucy took out the ashes and set the pan on the chalk line. Sam emptied them and brought back the pan. Lucy made up the whole bed, but she made it up from her own side. Sam kept his half of the house swept. He was a tidy man. Neither of them crossed that line.

Folks laughed about the queer arrangement, at first. Then they didn't laugh any more. They said it was a shame, and something dreadful would come of that mulishness and hatefulness between man and wife. They said it gave the town a bad name. At last they accepted the divided house and forgot all about it, except when strangers came and they wanted something to talk about.

"Yes, sir! They ain't said a single word to each other going on seven years."

The marketing was the hardest. Lucy could have written out a list of what she wanted. But she was too proud to, and Sam was too proud to ask her.

It was the cat, Calvin Coolidge, that saved the situation. He was getting old and housebound now. He was always curled up by the stove. Lucy would lean down and stroke him.

"Well, Calvin, I have my mouth all made up for liver this week. Don't you think a pound of liver would go good? And a pound of onions?"

Sam would bring the liver and onions that evening.

"Baked smelts would just about hit the spot tonight. Don't you hanker for them, Calvin?"

Sam got his baked smelts.

The two people did all their talking through the cat. They found the way around their stubbornness, for living's sake. They both loved the tomcat. It got easier and easier to talk through him.

"Calvin, do you suppose my oil-pants could be mended? They have a tear in the leg. And if I get wet out in the dory, I can't bring you home any tom-cods."

"I need saleratus and a spool of thread something awful, Calvin. If I don't get any thread, I can't sew any pants. If I don't have saleratus, I can't make you any biscuits, Calvin."

They got along through the years. Some people smiled. Some people felt more like crying. If they had had a child, it would have been different. A child could have saved them from ruining their lives.

The man and wife got so they seemed happy and natural. Sam loved to whistle at night. Lucy loved *Juanita* best of all the tunes. Sam whistled *Juanita* to Calvin Coolidge so often, the tomcat must have known it by heart. Lucy used to read the newspaper aloud to Sam. Now she read it every night to the cat as she held him on her lap and rocked back and forth in her Boston rocker.

But Calvin was getting on. He was getting so old he could hardly get about without running into things. All his gimp and fire were gone. It kind of frightened Lucy. It kind of scared Sam. They both thought how it was going to be with no cat to keep company through.

But the cat saved them a month before he died.

It was a night in February, blowing mean. Sam did the carelessest thing he had done since he was half-a-man-high. He left the last smelt he had yanked out of Blackwater River right on the hook when he put up his line in the corner. He was eating supper. All at once there came a great hullabaloo behind him. He jumped up.

It was Calvin. Hungry for fish, he had gulped the smelt on the line, hook and all. He was hanging from the line, howling. His eyes were balls of fire.

"Godfrey Diamonds!"

"Land of love!"

Sam was there in one jump. Lucy was there in two.

"Hold his paws still, Lucy, and I'll back the barb out of his mouth."

The tomcat bit and scratched. But Lucy held his paws firm. Sam worked the hook out. Calvin sputtered in fear. But he was all right. Lucy ran for the milk. She turned it out into a saucer. She filled the saucer and half the floor. For she had suddenly discovered she was on Sam's side of the house, and Sam was over on hers, rummaging for the iodine for her scratches.

Lucy went right over to the table. She took Sam's plate up and put it right down beside hers. She spoke sharply.

"Come finish your supper, Sam."

Sam came. He looked once at his plate, once at Lucy. Then he grinned. He did not say a word. He sat down beside his wife just as though it had been only eight minutes and not eight years.

"Eighteen cents a dozen was plenty for them pullets' eggs," Lucy said. And, a little bit later, "Aunt Sarah's eyes *were* kind of like an adder's."

They slept on Sarah's side of the bed that night.

A famous town landmark was gone for good.

15. Apple John

His name was Jonas. But no one ever called him that. It was an old *Bible* name that never did fit this unbiblical man who lived each year through for the amber cider at the golden end of it. He was Apple John, plain and simple. Sometimes people played games with his nickname and made it Demijohn—Demi, for short.

But Demijohn did not mind. The demijohn was his glory

and his cross. He was proud of it, in both capacities. The old-fashioned straw-covered jug was his solace and constant companion at the year's thin end. He lived with it for three months, from the coming in of the first wild yellow cider-apples to the going out of the last red astrachans looming through the snows over against the season of Thanksgiving. And Demi spent the other nine months of his year repenting and deploring his sinful three months of apples. The demijohn was his Lucifer and his evil master. And it brought him the only mellowness and happiness he had. When the sun was low, it was the only sunlight that fell on his aged days.

Lonely and queer as they come, Cider John, as he was also called, never married, never buried or recognized any of his relations, never owned roof overhead or acre underfoot, and never paid taxes. He was shaky in his wits. He talked to himself. He walked with an odd give to his knees, too light to be right. He was light-fingered. He was a thief. He lived off his neighbors, lived off the country, lived off the orchards of the score of small farms on my bay.

Apple felt he had as much right to any apple tree growing, to turn into cider, as any Red Indian had a right to any man's ash tree, to make his ancestral arrows of. There was a lot of the Red Man in Demijohn. He had the bitter Abenaki blood under his high, lean cheekbones, people said. And what blood besides ran in his narrow body was the blood of pioneer settlers, to whom all growing things were common property. So he went out on the full and the quarters and the dark of

[179]

the moon and sacked the likeliest apples, toted them home on his back, and manufactured them up in his hand-press—borrowed from my father—into the nectar that brought back the fire of the sun to the sad Autumnal days of the farmers of my seacoast.

The man's house was a piano-box, which had brought music into our family from far-away Chicago in the form of an upright piano. It stood well away from all the houses in the community. It leaned up against my father's biggest orchard, the Old Indian one, a mile from our house, growing in the heart of a white-pine-woods. Apple's only property, besides the borrowed hand-press he forgot to return, was a dozen five-gallon demijohns, upholstered in wicker. It was all the property he needed. For out of it flowed his living, his lust, and his repentance.

This lean squatter sold his year's harvest, demijohn by demijohn, as fast as it aged, and it aged quickly. He had the dark secret of hardening cider. He hardened it fast, and he disposed of it fast, and went back to the orchards roundabout for more of the makings. Envious rivals spied on Cider John, to come by his secret. Some said it was all done with yeast-cakes. But they never could do it with them. Others said it was a kind of small wild mushroom Apple put in. But they used every sort they could find, and even young toadstools, as one very sick man had to admit. But no one ever mastered the mystery. Men had to go back sheepishly and plank down the new dollar-bill on the demijohn, set out empty there under the hollow beech, for more of the same. A dollar was Apple's price for five gallons of flame and frenzy and glory. And they had to return the jug to the hollow beech, a small boy's cry from Apple's piano-box mansion.

Apple never took anything but a crisp new bill. He scorned money that had been tainted by handling and soiled by trade. He left any old bill on the jug's nose, and the jug remained empty below it. The town bank did a rushing business in new one-dollar bills in apple season. When a brand-new dollar was pinned down by the stopper, the jug filled up at once with the brew.

The wisest men said maybe it was the Indian strain in the apples and maybe Apple John knew what branches the Indian strains grew on, and so he could turn a mere juice into a deity with war-paint on and feathers in its hair. Anyway, there Demi's deity was, night after night, cramped up in a jug, waiting to get out and fill up the sky, waiting to make old men young, young men wise, and dumb men into middling-good baritones and good tellers of tales. And the new dollar was gone.

No one ever saw Cider John deliver a demijohn. No one ever saw him take a dollar. But the dollars came in, and the demijohns went out, regular as the stars' rising, in the Fall of the year. Wives would have given much to drag Demi to justice, in this land where Neal Dow's teetotalism had fastened itself like a blight on society for lo these many years. Yet no wife ever apprehended Apple with his illicit goods.

And husbands sang and told gay stories, men renewed their youth like the eagle, male society unbent around the cracker-barrel and the checker-board on all the Autumnal nights.

And Cider John unbent and renewed himself like the eagle and the young serpent, too. He unbent all over our upper pasture. He cast the nine months of virtue from him as a snake sheds his old skin in the Spring. We boys could hear the vast song Apple made under the harvest moon, the hunting moon, the moon of the falling leaves. He filled the whole farm full of music up to the brightly blazing Autumn stars. We could hear him, neighbors could hear him. Here was a maker of magic who was his own best customer. For every demijohn he sold, Cider John drank a whole one himself. Even-handed justice—demijohn for demijohn. That was his way of striking a balance with life. I cannot think of a better way to ensure excellence in a product, by the way. Require the producer to consume half of his product himself!

I cannot see the bright stars of any October night, to this day, but I hear, across the years, an old man singing like a dying swan. It was *In the Bay of Biscay-O, Barcelona Rose,* or *Whisky for My Johnny.* One of the three. That was the whole repertory of Apple. You can see why his *Bible* name did not become him. But whichever song it was, Demijohn poured it out full among the high and glittering stars. There were cracks in his aged voice, but the cider filled them pretty well in.

And it wasn't that Apple's cider was really hard. Not in

the way farmers measure hardness in cider. Whatever the code or the herb was that had transfigured it, the magic was quick magic, and the liquor had the bloom of youth and the must of the apples still upon it. It was not old, and it did not bite. It was young and tender, and it ran along the tongue like a strand of new silk.

You may wonder why this maker of cider whose house leaned upon our old orchard bothered to go to other people's trees for his apples. It was partly because Apple never depended upon one tree of apples or one orchard of them. He mixed his fruit up. That, I knew from my own boyish spying, was a part of his secret. But it was also partly because the wild *genii* of the woods were in this man. He went far afield and stole artistically because of the adventure in the thing.

Apple went by night always. And farmers might listen, might sit up by the kitchen window all night with their shotguns on their laps, but they never saw Apple, never heard rustle of a leaf. The thin old man went up the boughs like a blacksnake to a robin's nest. And he slithered down again with his sackful of booty and melted away into the forest without snapping a twig. Dawn, and the tree was stripped of its fruit. Demi never shook his apples down. He made no minute thunder of falling fruit to betray him. He picked his apples by hand, one by one. And he never touched a windfall or a spiked or specked apple in the years that I knew him.

This snake of the orchards ceased being a human being

[183]

when the cider season was in swing. He spoke to nobody. Nobody saw him go or come. He vanished from men's eyes. He was nowhere. But each man's demijohn was full the morning after he left his new dollar. Apple John was at work.

Apple was at work like a beaver, I could see, though I could not see Apple. I watched his house from afar. He had an enormous fire up. The smoke poured from the stovepipe that stuck out of one of his four panes. Fire must have entered into the cider secret somewhere, somehow, I shall always believe. Either that, or else Apple heated his thin old blood up to get the proper underholds on deity! And I could see the cider coming all right. It was coming out of Apple's sink-spout like a thick strand of amber silk and running into the ground. Not into the ground really, but into a half-hogshead Cider John had purloined from father and buried in the earth under his spout. I had investigated, boy-fashion, when Apple was in town. I knew all about that half-hogshead. Demi never once came out. But the cider did. I watched it flow for hours. At a distance.

I always kept my distance when the cider season was on Demijohn. In other months he countenanced my presence, though he never invited it, and he told me wry old tales of life hereabouts sixty and seventy years before I was born. He told me the hair-raising tale of the old cellar-hole right near his cabin. It was where a house stood that was burned down by the Indians, and a little girl hid herself in the well down

[184]

in that cellar and heard and saw the house burn over her head, heard her people scream as they were scalped. The water kept her cool and alive. As a boy, Apple knew that girl as a bent old woman. He had the story from her lips. Apple John told me the story because, nine months of the year, he was my friend.

But the other three months, when it was apples he loved, Apple John broke off his friendship, and I did not dare come as close to him as a crow's call. So I could not tell just what went on in that hogshead underground. I would have given anything to. But I did not dare go close and see. The earth was banked around it, everywhere except at one side, where the bunghole was. Apple kept the bunghole open so he could get the cider out, when it was finished with its working in the coolness of the earth. The earth had something to do with the secret. I know that for sure.

It was the only time the old man was happy. I knew that also. Three months of happiness. It is more than most men can ask out of any year. Everyone knew Apple was happy. They heard him being happy, nights! He had his art, his secret, and his annual sin. What more could a man want? They were all Apple asked. He wanted no part of human society and humanity then.

Yet, when the snow began to fly and only the sour crab-apples were left on the bare apple boughs, the nights up there in our old orchard quieted down, the song stopped, the demijohns went back empty sans the dollar-bill and disappeared, and Apple John came back to civilization. Not very far back. Only within spitting distance. But he came. The old fellow came stumbling into our yard to borrow our second-best cart and horse to go to town and buy his Winter's provisions. The old blacksnake was gone. It was just an old man whose knees creaked and who had patches on his knees. He was small and shrunken in his old clothes, this man. His old eyes ran rheum. He was not the thing I had seen slide like a slim deity through the woods on an October twilight. He got his victuals in town—salt pork and cornmeal—and settled down to his nine months of sadness and his repentance of his great and single and god-like sin.

Demi knew cider was his sin. He told the Methodist testimonial meetings about it, Sunday nights. He asked his Creator's forgiveness for making men stumble in the way, and stumble into a glory and sing, for stumbling himself and singing in the way, too. It was a genuine sorrow. He wept tears of remorse. I, a small boy, saw them glisten down his leathery cheeks. I saw them in the Methodist light from the four reflector-lamps. He was the son of Satan, the minion of Beelzebub. The Old Boy, he confessed, was in him, bigger than a woodchuck. Would his Creator forgive him, this once more?

I hope his Creator did. For just as sure as September rolled around again, red and golden with maples and apples, Apple John rolled around again, too. And sang. He dared disobey

his Creator once more. He got out the demijohns and his
sack. He vanished out of day and lived only at night. He
worked unseen in his little house, the smoke poured through
the pane, and the ribbon of silky cider started coming out of
the sink-spout and into the buried half-hogshead. Nights
again ran over with song. In Active I. Jones's corner-store,
in the pinewoods of our upper pasture. And the Creator probably began to get ready for the annual forgiveness to come.

The nine months of our year Apple had no joy, only sorrow and sackcloth. But the last three of the year he abun-
dantly lived. That was when he was most alive.

Except for one little thing. On one silver-lettered night, on
the other side of the year, I caught Apple John more alive
than ever among the apples.

It was a windy April night, there was a watery moon, and
the silver of it lay on the swollen maple buds. I had been out
late looking for mayflowers in the swamp below the Old
Orchard. I hadn't found any. And now I was hot-footing it
home to a late supper and a scolding through a world ringing
with silvery peepers and silvered all over with that watery
full moon. I came around the fallen tree in the Old Indian
Orchard, and I stopped as though I had been struck by the
moon. Someone was at the top of the oldest apple tree there.
I held my breath.

It was Apple John. And he had a knife in his hand, and it
flashed little flames in the moon. I saw what he was up to.

He was setting a scion to the old apple bough. I knew, from watching my father. He was grafting our old tree. I was near enough so I heard Apple, how he talked to himself fast, excitedly, low down in his throat. I could not make out what he was saying. At times he whistled queerly through his snag-teeth. He was fearfully excited. I could hear him taking in deep breaths. I did not move a muscle. I waited a long time, watching. Then suddenly, the tree was empty. Without my seeing him do it, Apple John had slithered from the boughs and had melted into the night.

My father had wondered for years what made those old trees of ours in Indian Orchard keep on bearing so, what made the apples on them seem to change so from year to year. Now I knew why.

And in the years after that night I saw this old hermit, who lived by himself and talked to himself more and more as all his teeth left him and he bent lower to the ground, graft apple tree after apple tree in all the orchards along the coast. Always by night. Always on the full of the moon. I never told a soul what I saw. I thought it was not right to. I did not know then what unholiness really meant. But I knew that telling on the old man would be just that and nothing more.

Somehow, old Apple John's cider secret was tied in with that secret grafting he did, under the Spring moons. He was paying nature back, even if he did not pay men, for his theft of the apples, for his secret sin.

One late Fall night at last, at the end of the apple season,

Apple John disappeared. He faded into the night, stayed there, and never returned.

We saw a glow on the sky over the Old Orchard. We thought it was the Northern Lights. In the morning, though, we were up there, my father and I, and we saw it hadn't been Northern Lights at all. It had been Apple John's house. It was burned flat to the ground.

We poked among the cinders gingerly, grimly, silent both of us. My father's eyes were brimming full. I knew what he expected to find. He expected to find bones. He did. But they were only the bones of a half dozen or so of our sheep that had disappeared one by one, year by year, that Apple had hidden under his floor. There were no other bones. My father straightened up and smiled. He was glad even in spite of the sheep. Apple must have got out of the bonfire he had set by upsetting his lamp over the last demijohn of the year.

The glass of the demijohns was there. Twisted and melted. The buried half-hogshead was warped in its staves, singed, and empty. It made us kind of sad.

Well, Apple John could fix everything up again next year. He would come around later in the day, wanting some new boards for a house and home.

But Apple didn't. He never came around again. No one ever laid eyes on him. Where he wandered off to nobody knew. I thought of what had become of the old horse we had that wandered off into the swamp one Winter. We found the bones in Spring.

[189]

My father's face grew long. He wondered if he knew his "boneology." He looked again. They were sheep bones, all right.

Today not one in a thousand people remember that man of the apples, maker of cider. He has no relation left. He has faded out of all talk. He is gone for good.

Yet everywhere, among the gnarled old orchards of my coast country, on apple trees that should have sunk into the earth-mold by rights a hundred years ago, people come on boughs, young as ever, still laden down with fruit each Fall. Not the pampered, weakling apples men raise in these years, but apples such as our ancestors bit into, and the Indians before them. Governor Dunlops, Greensleeves, and Wintersets. Famous old hardy fruits almost forgotten by horticulture now.

These tough apples make the finest cider there is.

I guess the Creator forgave Apple John after all. I guess Apple sort of evened things up with him.

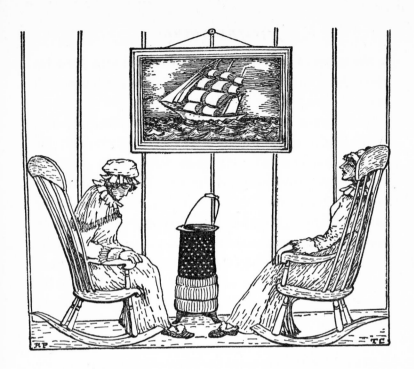

16. The Captains Rolled Over
in Their Graves

ANNIE was soft, but Zenobia, her sister, was hard as the Rock of Gibraltar.

The Quinnam girls, as coast people called them, were in their eighties now. They were spinsters and kept house together in the old sea-captain mansion of the family. They were the last of a generation that had seen great ships grow up from a keel and slide down through Maine daisies, on their way to Batavia and Singapore and Rio. People said the two girls must rattle around in so big a house.

Zenobia was the strong one. She had always had to do Annie's thinking for her all her life. Annie was afraid of her own shadow, afraid of putting in too much tea in the teapot, afraid to call her soul her own. Zenobia had to do everything about the house, and hoe the garden and do the shopping in town, too. She couldn't trust Annie even to build the fire.

Zenobia had the strength of ten. She had kept everything ship-shape in the Quinnam House for going on eighty years. The old sea captains of the family could have eaten off her floors. Not that they would have needed to, if they had come back from the bottom of the Indian Ocean or the South Pacific. There were scrubbed tables enough for them to eat a meal of victuals on. Zenobia never allowed a spider to spread a web or a spot to smutch her wallpapers. Everything was spick-and-span and Bristol-fashion.

Of course, as she and her sister got deeper into the sunset, Zena had had to take in her sails a bit. For Annie's sake, she had come to sleeping double. Annie's bones, for all her fleshiness, felt the cold so. And Zena had had to come downstairs, to the room next the sitting-room. It was a terrible New England comedown. But that was where they slept.

And Annie was so soft, Zenobia had made the concession of having a fire in the sitting-room, to warm her sister up

[192]

before she plunged into the icy sheets. It was as near to the sin of sleeping in a warmed room as Zena could come. But she came. She toasted her own shins, too, of course, while Annie warmed hers, so as not to waste the fire. But she could have done without it. She had done without all her life.

It was only an oil-stove Zenobia lighted for the bed-going. She brought it in by its tall handle and set it down in the middle of the room. Then she and Annie undressed around it, and sat in their nightgowns for a bit. Afterwards, they got up and dived together into the cold bed.

It had been like using pages of the family *Bible* for tapers, their undressing in the sitting-room. But Annie was soft. Zena had had to come to it. Her ancestors, the hard old captains, must be turning over in their watery graves!

This January night was cracking cold. The blue stars sputtered at the windows. It was too cold for the panes to frost up. It was away below zero. The water bucket in the kitchen was skimming over. Annie and Zenobia had their long flannel nightgowns on, and they were sitting in their rocking-chairs, with the hot oil-stove exactly in between them. Annie kept dozing off, as she always did. Zenobia had to keep an eye on her all the time.

"Annie! You're asleep! Wake up!"

Annie's plump pink face came up with a start in the light coming like polka-dots from the holes in the stove. "I'm sorry, Zena."

The oil-stove made a purring sound like a cat. Zena hadn't

had a cat for years. The house was awful still. It was a shame to waste all this oil. But the heat felt good on Zena's knees. It was kind of nice. No cat for years. It was like having a cat right on her lap. Like . . .

Zenobia's chin jerked up. She sat up with a guilty jump. She had napped. She looked across at Annie. Her mouth fell open wide. Her blood froze in her.

There was no Annie there! Annie had gone. A large fat negress had stolen in. And there she sat in Zenobia's best chair! Her horrible black face lolled over in the dim light.

Zenobia let out a blood-curdling scream.

Her mother had been frightened half out of her wits once by a vast negro her husband had brought home from the Barbadoes. The fright had marked Zenobia before she was born.

Zenobia let out a louder scream.

Annie came to. Her eyes popped open. She saw a fearful thing. A tall negress had her mouth open and was yowling at her like a terrible alley cat. The only bright parts to her were two rolling white eyes and an immense red mouth.

Annie shrieked in mortal terror. She yelled and yelled and could not stop.

When Zenobia saw the vast mouth in the sleeping negress gape open, and when she saw her eyes roll back to nothing but the whites, she let out scream on scream on scream.

The two of them sat and screamed together. The house quivered.

The neighbors came running. When they burst in the door,

[194]

they saw a sight that staggered them. The Quinnam sisters, black as coals, sat facing each other in their chairs, and they were screaming in each other's face like all Bedlam broken loose.

The oil-stove had gone on a rampage while Zenobia dozed. It had smoked up. It had filled the room with floating carbon. It had turned two white New England spinsters into women of the Inner Congo. There they sat, screaming at each other.

It took the neighbors ten minutes to calm the sisters down. It wasn't until they brought wash-cloths and got their faces white that the sisters stopped taking on. Zenobia was worse than Annie. She was still crying out after Annie was just sobbing and hiccupping.

It was nearly cockcrow by the time the neighbors had got Annie and Zenobia clean New England folks again. They had to scrub them all over with soap and get them new night-gowns. They had to pat them and stroke their hair. They had them soothed down at last and side by side in the clean bed. But even then, Zenobia the hard, Zenobia the strong, was weeping like a child.

The sitting-room was black as Egypt. It would take weeks of scrubbing to get the soot off the walls and ceiling. Some of it would never come out. Some of it is still there to this day in the plaster and wood.

And from that night on, Zenobia Quinnam showed a streak of gentleness in her at last. She gave in and let Annie sleep

in a warm room. She brought the bed out into the sitting-
room and put it right smack up against the brand-new air-
tight wood-stove she bought for them to sleep with, nights.

Maybe the old captains rolled completely over in their
Pacific graves.

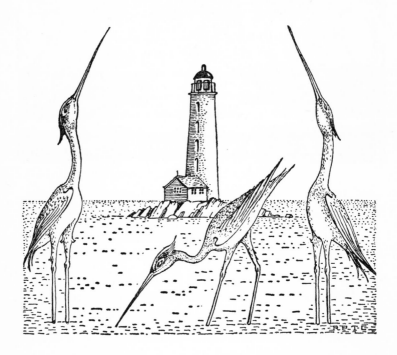

17. My Father's Henchmen

MY FATHER was cut out for a mead-hall. I mean, he was cut out on the old Anglo-Saxon lines, and he simply had to have a houseful of henchmen around him. He had to have his retainers. A meal, for him, was a score of hearty men dipping their thick moustaches in his soup and making the floor timbers of his kitchen groan with their avoirdupois. It was stories and songs, too, in the ancient mead-hall manner, after the marrowbones had all been split and the hounds had relaxed their limbs under the table. My father led the stories and songs. He was the king-pin man at them both. And a meal with him was a dozen starry-eyed children, sandwiched in between the broad bases of the family retainers, and listening all wide ears to the lord of the manor, and their creator, telling such ghost stories that they fell asleep with their faces in their plates, for fear of going off into the dark to bed, and joined the hounds in dreams while the stars slipped over half of the sky.

If it wasn't uncles—and we had an assorted plenty of them—it was hired-men. Them we had in legions.

We didn't need hired-men. Our farm was a fairly small one, in arable land. Two grown men worked to disadvantage on our beanfields tucked into the folds of the ledges. They got in each other's way. Our hired-men got tangled all up. Sometimes they were three deep on the smallest job. Lord knows there were boys of us enough to do most of the chores. And the kind of hired-men we had were perfectly willing to let us boys do them. They applauded us and egged us on. They bet on one boy against the others. I don't know how many cord-feet of beechwood I manufactured up to save some stalwart man a quarter, and win his approbation and one penny.

Father had to keep busy all the time trying to find something for a platoon of henchmen to do, and when he found it, they farmed it right out on us, often as not. But father had to have men around him. He liked them big, like himself. Our hired-men ran very big. Most of them ran to over fifteen stone, as the British like to measure man, by the fourteen-pound lots. And they were like stone, too, on our chairs and benches. They wore them right down in hollows. It was hard for small boys to fit their cushions to the hollows worn in cane and pine by stout men. The men were hard on floors also. Of course, they were good for the smaller fry to practice mountain climbing on. They made admirable horses, too, in tournaments. We boys found good use for them even when father couldn't.

But the henchmen we had had to be handled with white kid gloves. For they were New England hired-men. And New England hired-men are a very special order of creation, let me tell you. They rank far above uncles as creatures requiring special treatment. Our men even ranked above aunts. Next to the head of the house, they had to have the best. All plans had to rotate about them. They had to have certain chairs to sit in. They had to have special beds. They had to have their water at a certain heat for the Saturday night bath. And even then many of them did not take it. We boys could never get by Saturday night without a bath. But our hired-men could. And did. They gloried in their freedom from the family rules and *mores*. They refused to go to church on the Sabbath.

All except Ezekiel. He insisted on going to three. And we had to deliver him there. Universalist, Baptist, and Meth-

odist—in that order. He had to take in all three, to feel saved.
The Universalist and Baptist came at the same time, but
Ezekiel halved himself between them. Methodism came at
night, and Ezekiel abandoned himself to it for two hours.
He abandoned himself to most religions. He had to have
them to get along. He was a vast man, he stood six-feet, seven
or eight, and he took a vast lot of religion to fill up all the
corners in his frame. He had to soak up enough religion on
a Sunday to last him the week. Religion was what kept him
going strong.

"Glory to God!" Ezekiel would shout, when they led him
out to a big woodpile Monday morning. Then he spat on his
anchors of hands and sailed into the oakwood. He was a
simple man, but he knew the Creator liked to hear a bucksaw screech. Zeke made his sing. He kept his bucksaw red-
hot.

"Glory! Glory to God!" he would bellow so people could
hear him two farms away. He shouted his way through a
cord of red oak or white beech by dinner time. Then he came
in and fell on the victuals just as hard. He ate voluminously.
He ate a pot of baked beans at a sitting. "Glory to God!"
Then he ate a pot of baked peas right on top of that. And
he washed both pots down with a whole quart pitcher of
molasses. "Glory! Glory!" And out he ran to another cord
of wood they had got together for him during dinner. He
ran from cord to cord. It was worth filling him full of religion on Sunday, he ate through the week's wood so. Har-

nessed to three kinds of religion, he kept the whole houseful of strong men in superb heat. He was our running hired-man.

Most of our hired-men were walkers, though. They took their sweet time about getting from task to task. Especially in salt-haying time. And I didn't blame them for that.

Salt-hay! The blisters come out on me in memory when I remember that, on my hands, on my feet, on other projections of me.

Ours was an amphibious farm. It was as much ocean and tidal mud as land. Our cows were amphibious cows. Sea-going cows. They hankered for the hay that grows under the tide. They craved lots of salt. So my father provided them with it. Salt-hay is under the sea at high tide, but at the ebb, unfortunately, it emerges. And that was when we surprised it and cut it. It had to be cut fast, by hand, and it had to be carried fast out of the tide's way, by hand also. By the hired-men's hands and the boys'. My father did the cutting. The rest of us did the lugging. We carried the wet, heavy stuff on hand-bars and spread it on the beaver dams, to make. The black-flies and mosquitoes stung our eyes to, while our hands strained at the bars. We mired ourselves in the mud to our ears. When the hay had dried, we piloted the horses out on the dams and tried to navigate the rack astraddle the beavers' mountains. Almost invariably our horses, just as we got the rack completely loaded, slipped off the dams and sank out of sight, all but their heads. Then the hired-men and we boys rigged tackle-and-fall and mined the horses from the mud. It was as much mining as haying.

No one could blame our henchmen for going slow at such work. My father didn't. Our hired retainers went slow as cold molasses on even the hottest days. They husbanded their strength artfully. I think they purposely led the horses on to the soft places, to get themselves a breathing space and a chance to sit down and slap the mosquitoes off themselves. The horses didn't mind being mired at all. They were insulated from the mosquitoes and the green-head horseflies all the time they were in the earth. They munched the daisies on the beaver dams above them, the ones they could reach, and lay at utter peace.

While we boys were resting between loads, the hired-men let us turn the grindstone for father's scythe. I came through my overalls every day with going around with that lopsided stone hour after hour while my hands turned into blisters.

The sweet-haying was easier going. But it presented about the same combination of problems of using too many men on too little hay. It took all the tact and finesse my father had to keep the hired-men interested and entertained at the job.

If it hadn't been for the kind of mowing-machine we had, I doubt if even my sire could have kept our hired-men thinking that the haying was worth their while. Our mowing-machine intrigued them and provided them with constant adventure. It was a Worcester Buckeye, the first one built, I think, dating from about the time of the Civil War. Anyway, it was unique. There were no others left in the world like it. So there were no replacements for its parts. Each trip around the field it lost a good many of its essentials. Those of us boys and men who were not driving the horses from on foot, or ballasting down the seat to keep the mower's wheels on the ground, followed along behind the machine and picked up the pieces as they came off. The machine spilled cogs and springs and housings everywhere. At the end of each swath, we rested the horses and tried to fit the mechanical jigsaw puzzle together again. Some parts we had not found, of course, and replacements for those we had to make up out of old cookstoves and harrows and plows. Always, too, there were a lot of parts we could find no place for. But the hired-men loved all this monkeying with our Buckeye. It gave them a chance to play blacksmith and carpenter and inventor, repairing it. They loved the old thing passionately. And it gave them magnificent chances for rest.

Our hired-men were artistic resters. They had to be, with so little work for so many. If they hadn't rested a great deal, they would have wound up all the day's work by nine o'clock in the morning, and would have run right out of a job.

Take John Jensen, now. He was the greatest artist among our hired resters. He rested so often and so long that resting became permanent with him. He rested so much that every pair of pants the man had to his name wore through at the seat while the creases were still in the front of the legs. He was the kind of man who could rest even when he was shingling the barn. He could sleep and use his shingling hatchet, too. He had mastered the technique so that he could drive the nails in his dreams. There he sat on the roof with his Swedish moustaches flaring out each way like the smellers on an insect over the enormous mouthful of nails he had taken in below. And with both eyes closed in sleep he spat out the nails one by one, caught each without looking, and gave it a clip with his hatchet. Of course, he missed every other nail. The nails went off over the barn into the pine-woods with a happy *zing*. But John Jensen did not mind. He never struck twice at a nail, never hit twice in the same place. He hitched right along on his proud patches and tried again, with a new shingle. And when the wind came up strong, the shingles he had missed nailing blew off the roof. So there still was a job of shingling for Jensen to do. He was a per-petual shingler. He spent his life, practically, on our barn. It was a good thing, for being built like a Viking, he was too heavy, as my father put it, for light work. The shingles were light, but they didn't matter.

Then there was old Amos. He was light-fingered. Every-body knew Amos took things that did not belong to him. But everybody knew he couldn't help it and respected his weak-ness. It was a colorful thing that had to be allowed for. My mother put up two extra jars to every dozen of preserves be-cause she knew Amos would steal that many. Fourteen jars in every dozen. And she sent us boys up to collect the empties, in Amos's shack, when he was through with them and she needed them.

My father had to lay in extra trousers to cover Amos's nakedness. Amos was negligent of his appearance. My father had to put the extra pants practically under Amos's feet before he could get Amos to steal them and dress himself right. My father would gladly have given Amos his pants. But that would have taken the wind out of Amos's sails and defeated his sense of sufficiency, and he would have been no good at hoeing the turnips. He was a good hoer, when he had his pride. Take his pride away from him, and he was a poor one. He had to have his thievery to keep him going full sail. The other men said Amos stole even from himself. I think he did, for he was always taking plugs of his own chewing tobacco—which he stole from father—and hiding them in places where he could never find them.

All our retainers had their little eccentricities, and these had to be respected.

With Al Snow it was song. Al could not really carry a tune. Yet he was always trying to. He got all the words right, but they came out all alike in sound. He sang all the time—he had to, to work right. It was a disturbing thing until you got used to it. Then you made allowance for it and never noticed it at all.

Sam Will's eccentricity was women. I could not understand many of the details, being too young to get them straight at the time. But I remember hearing father and everybody else saying that women were Sam's Paris-green.

Hen Wright was off center on drink. From Friday noon to Monday noon, he was just not to be counted on. He was not even to be seen. With him it was a case of total immersion or nothing. He went to his room over the toolshed, and did not emerge till Monday at dinner time. Then he came in, thin as a rail, to eat.

All our henchmen did one thing superbly. That was eating. Being big men, they needed a lot to go on. My mother had to have a number of retainers in skirts, in the kitchen, to keep my father's retainers in trousers going. They ate long, and they ate a lot.

The chief thing to be considered in cooking for our New England brand of hired-men was bulk, and after that, color. They ran to things like red-flannel hash. Mountains of it. Subtlety was not called for. A heaping platter of home-fried potatoes, mahogany-brown, was more to them than the finest roast of mutton. They did not crave variety. They were men of small range, but they wanted that range stout. They demanded their plain pork and potatoes done the same way, year in and year out, and they wanted heaping platters of them.

Pork-gravy was the staple they clamored for loudest. They could make a whole meal off it and do days of haying of our amphibious kind with nothing more than this to maintain them—with ten or so bushels of plain boiled Irish potatoes to pour the pork-gravy over, or, say, several bushels of plain boiled fresh cod.

Pork-gravy, the elixir of old New England, is an easy dish to concoct. You cut a chunk of salt pork into thin strips and fry them till they are brown. You mix up a thickening as you would for soup—two tablespoons of water to two of flour —and stir out all the lumps. Then you simply put your two halves of the dish together, mixing the thickening in with the pork scraps and pork fat seething on the hot stove. Let the whole business boil, stirring till it thickens up. Then bring out your potatoes and codfish—or better still, both—and blow the horn for the hired-men.

Our hired-men could hear the pork-gravy horn ten miles from the farmhouse, in a gale of wind. They came running. It was the only time they came running. Except Glory-to-God Ezekiel. He was always running from one woodpile to the next as well as from woodpile to pork-gravy and back. Ezekiel ate two spiders full of pork-gravy at one sitting— balanced with five pounds of fresh cod, of course—and never batted an eye.

Our retainers liked shad, in season. But they wanted no fine spices or fixings on it. They wanted it fried and fried and fried. Plain. With pork-scraps. They ate it by the slab, blowing out the bones from under the awnings of their thick moustaches—what bones they could bother with, the big ones; the rest they swallowed. In shad season, when the farm was crowded by the fish, our men found it hard to undress at night, they said. It was one of their jokes. They had eaten so many shad bones that the bones had come out on their skins, and their shirts stuck to them tight.

Dundee pudding was the favorite supper of our men. And don't think this pudding was merely the dessert. It was the whole meal. My mother started the pudding off on the base she started most hired-men dishes on: fried salt pork. She fried the scraps brown on the bottom of her kettle. Then she put in three pints of water, added half a cup of black molasses, and brought it all to a boil. After that, she took a sieve full of cornmeal and sifted it into a pan. Handful by handful she threw the sifted meal into the kettle of boiling water, stirring hard to break up the lumps. When it was good and thick, so the spoon would almost stand alone in it, she set the kettle on the back of the stove and let the thing cook for a quarter of an hour. The men marched in and ate the pudding hot, washing it down with cold milk till they were fit to founder. And what the men did not eat that night, like King Arthur in the old nursery rhyme, they got next morning for breakfast, fried. Mother sliced it cold and fried it in pork-fat. The men drenched it with cold molasses.

It was such a dish, the hired-men swore, as would put whiskers on a brass monkey. Our retainers always identified whiskers with strength. They were heavily whiskered.

Of course, my father's henchmen had other uses than for

work. Oh, many others. We children used them for stories. No one else could tell us such lies.

We boys used them for making us toy boats, too. They could whittle hulls out of white pine and rig them up with mother's linen thread into ships that made a little boy dance till he split his breeches. They ran us up canoes out of pea-pods, putting in decks and small seats of different lengths of matches. One of them ran us up skiffs big enough for us to go spearing flounders in and capsize. They were great men with jack-knives. Give them a piece of dry white pine, and they would let the bunched hay stay out through three thunderstorms. They forgot they were men with moustaches on them and pants that came to the ground. They came down to our level, held their breaths in like small boys, and went on all fours among us, playing harder than any of us in short pants.

I think that was mostly the reason my father hired these men. He wanted his boys to have a good time and fine toys, and fine boy-companions. Our henchmen provided us with all three. It was worth paying any price having his boys' eyes shine as they did when Ezekiel or Hen or Amos turned out whole fleets of ships or Noah's arks full of zebras and elephants. Father smiled seeing such sights. And sooner or later, didn't he get right down on his knees and become one of us boys along with his hired-men!

IV

MAINE TABLE
IN FULL BLOOM

18. Pig Was Peak

THE pig was the peak. The year on the saltwater farm of
my colthood went up to a perfect summit made of fresh
pork. That was pig-sticking time, and it came around the
end of the year when frost was in the air and the last arrows
of wild geese were whizzing over towards Florida. It saved
those melancholy days from melancholy.

Of course, the pig was the prop on which our whole
Winter, Spring, and Summer leaned. He was the salty cornerstone of the baked beans, the beginnings of all the best

gravies; he made the string-beans of Summer rich and tasty; from his barrel in the cellar he came up at all seasons. Pig was the Fujiyama of all our days; wherever, whenever we looked up, we saw him. But it was his fresh, unsalted self—fattened on the rich overflow of Autumn till he couldn't see out of the corners of his china-blue eyes and so had no call to go on looking at scenery or life—that peaked up the pleasure of our eating to the stars, along about Thanksgiving time.

There was snow on this top to our year. There had to be. For it wasn't safe to knock the pigs over till the weather was cold enough to keep their carcasses from spoiling. So heavy frosts and snowflakes meant fresh meat at last. We were willing to see the leaves fall from the trees and the flowers wither on the stalk, willing to see the year die, because we now had the huge roses of pigs spread wide open out in the woodshed. If the rose petals were gone, there were the rose petals of pork chops filling our house with fresh fragrance. It was a fair swop.

Very few of the farm pigs survived that red-letter day on the November calendar when the grindstones sang, the sparks flew, and strong, tall men in long dusters, with a glint in the eye and a glinting knife in the hand, went into the pig-pen. Why the stickers wore long white coats I don't know. The good ones never needed any protection to their ordinary pants. I think it was a piece of ritualism.

We boys lived for the day. We were hard-hearted. Pigs that we boys had been fast friends with, when they had been

all baby-pink and innocent, now went squealing over the
Great Divide, and their late boy-companions danced up and
down for joy till they nearly burst seams in their breeches. It
was the penalty for reaching maturity too fast. It was a
punishment for the pigs' growing up ahead of us. For their
getting too fat too quickly. It was all in the stars that little
boys should be glad to see their four-footed friends die and
gentle big men turn into stern executioners, this one day in
the year. It couldn't be helped. The farm was hungry for
meat. The pigs were ripe. The weather was cold and propi-
tious. It was all the stars' doing. All of us must march up to
the brink some day. It was the pigs' turn. It was their
twilight.

A tense air of expectancy had been building up for days.
The pigs had been poured out extra pailfuls of gruel and
soured milk. They had been gorging themselves till they
couldn't run any more. They should have known that something was in the air. But pigs pay no attention to portents.
They have no concept of the sinister. Our pigs kept right on
stuffing themselves till they could barely grunt.

Out in the empty garden, frost crystals had been humping
the ground up higher and higher each morning. The wind
had a sharp edge to it. And suddenly the thin gray clouds
darkened and lowered, and a white thing zigzagged down.
Then a few more. Then a whole worldful. It was the hour.

Uncles had been gathering. Trust uncles to scent spare-ribs
miles and miles away! The woods were filling up with hun-

gry cousins with a lot of space in their clothes to fill. Grind-stones had been screaming. The knives had been ground till they shone like silver. Boys had gone to bed taut with excite-ment.

The pigs should have guessed something was up. But they hadn't. They did not suspect a thing even when the chill dawn found no gruel at all in their troughs. No breakfast at all. Yet no shadow darkened their small brains. They merely tipped back their snouts and squealed till the farm reeled. They were the lords of creation. They wanted their break-fast. They demanded it imperiously, so they could be heard four farms away.

What they got was cold steel.

The men in the long dusters came, right hand behind their backs, straddled over the fence into the pig-pen, and beck-oned with their left hand. "Come, piggy, piggy! Nice piggy." They fairly oozed gentleness. It was all right. The pigs were going to have their breakfast, after all. Come up to the nice gentleman and get it. The small boys leaned over the pen, and their breeches plumped out like so many pats of butter in a row. And piggy-piggy—the fool—came right up to the gentleman in the duster.

The next thing was lightning. It flashed out from behind the gentleman, and it hit the pig under the chin, where his neck—if he hadn't been greedy and a pig—should have been. It was quick and clean. But it was death. The pig bounced back on his hams, and he sat there dazed, trying to figure out what had happened to him. And all at once his life came out of him, red.

Squeals came out, too. Squeals on squeals, slanting up faster and faster to such high trebles that the ear could record them no more, and they faded out into silence. It was not like the squealing for breakfast, this. It was higher-pitched. It was the pure essence of dolorousness. It was the ultimate in squeals. It was the swan song of Peter Peabody Pig. When it was done, he was done.

I don't believe the pig really suffered very much. It was too quickly done. I believe the squeals he made were purely in the interest of art. I think he wanted to put on an artistic last act.

It was a noble ending the pig had. He fell like Achilles before a little sharp point, thin as an arrow. A slender thing brought him low. And he lay, after his un-Homeric squealing was out of him, like a king gone down. The executioner was an artist. He did not have to wipe his knife off. There was nothing on it to mar its brightness. It came out too quick. There was nothing on the man to spot his duster. He smiled to the boys, like a successful matador, and climbed out of the pen, spotless.

All but my Uncle Asa. He never emerged spotless. He emerged from the pen looking like St. Bartholomew's Eve. He came out all over gore, and part of it his own. And the poor pig was not finished. He was a writhing earthquake, erupting maledictions like a volcano. Other men had to jump

in and give him his *coup-de-grâce*. They had to take Uncle
Asa into the house, too, and wash him and pour in iodine
and alcohol—internally as well as into his skin—and bandage
him up. But Uncle Asa never learned. Not my Uncle Asa.
He came back smiling wide for the pig-sticking annually and
came annually to grief. So did the pig he picked out. It was
in the stars.

Once the squeals faded, the hog was dragged instantly by
his heels to the shed, followed by all the gallery of small boys.
There he was elevated on the great hook and doused head-
first into a hogshead of boiling water. Steam came up in
clouds, and the men there, with long knives, scraped his
bristles off his scalded skin in the twinkle of a Maine blue
eye. The pig was pink once more, as he had been as a baby.
And his eyes were squizzled shut in utter peace. Up he went
on the tackle-and-fall by his heels again, and a wide-shoul-
dered man with a blade like a Zulu spear, a man who knew
every secret a pig had in him, slashed this way, slashed that,
laid him wide open from snouted stem to pompous and
plump stern, from ring on the nose to the curlicue of his tail.
Everything came tumbling out of him—blue, green, gray,
brown works. The boys bugged their eyes. They had never
guessed a pig had so much to him. The haslet—heart, liver,
and company—was rushed to the house where the frying
pan was hissing and waiting.

I suppose there is some meat in the world as tasty as a
newly-butchered hog's liver. But I have never come across it.

Sea Captain's House

These crescent moons of brown meat, fried in hot fat along with bacon, and a few slivers of baby onion around them, eat like a dream of falling in love come true. They should be eaten with cream-o'-tartar biscuits, hot as they are, and yellow with country butter piled on deep. The liver of the pig is the first part of the pig to come to the table.

The next is spare-ribs. *O altitudo!*

Out in the shed the pig is hung high by his heels now, an oaken stick strung through his Achilles' tendons. He is clean as a cherub, all his sins washed away. He is spread open like a red butterfly, like a folio—delectable meat of every conceivable texture and taste, of every shading of fat and lean. There he will hang for days, while the smokehouse is being made ready for his hams, while the vats are being prepared for his sausage meat. The cold air laps him round with proof. He will be safe for weeks and months. For any breakfast, dinner, or supper, you will have to go no farther than the woodshed, you will need only to go out with your knife and cut your meal off.

But a pig's spare-ribs are the most fragile and dainty part of him—after his liver—and the magic of their flavor is briefer than a May-fly's life. So they should be rushed to the house, right on the heels of the liver, and baked at once brown as Winter oak leaves, and eaten by the farm people for dinner—dinner coming at noon, as it should where strong men live and work in the open air.

I don't think there is anything that can bring out the goodness in a man as new spare-ribs can. They are the ideal combination of the tenderest lean and the robustest fat. Their meat is everywhere married close to the bone, and the bones are delicate ones and like marrow itself. A strong man can eat the bones themselves if he is good and hungry. My Uncle Asa usually was. The technique of nibbling the meat from the bones, from east to west, as the sun travels, is an engrossing affair. I don't believe there is so much ecstasy this side of love-making as in following that meat along on, say, sixteen or seventeen slender floating ribs of a year-old pig, till your eyes light up like morning-glories, and the fat runs down your chin! There is no such comforting sight to a father as my father had when his boys and girls sat around that noonday table of ours with richness shining on their chins. And of course on father's chin, too. And on Uncle Asa's bandaged one. Ecstasy is the word! No wonder we burst into song. That old song of ours for that red-letter day of the pig's decease is pure exclamation points:

> O rare ribs! O spare-ribs!
> O ribs he couldn't spare!

Marrow and fatness were the best things the *Bible* promised. The pig-sticking season was when we felt most biblical of all.

Of course there were a hundred other delights and dishes to follow. That is the great advantage to a pig. He is so many contrasting and provoking parts and so many possibilities that you never grow weary of him. Not the way you would of a sheep or a rooster. He has over a hundred surprises packed away in his pampered body. Two for every week in the year.

We went on next to the pig's tail. Or rather father did. That fell properly to father. It was his right, by virtue of being your begetter. He ate it, curled up with an air of finality, fried. And he nibbled off the meat on every vertebra!

We children and the rest were for the pig's head, meantime. In a white-hot oven Mother roasted the biggest head of the several pigs that had squealed their November last. She put potatoes around, the farm's best, and onions, and thickened the dish, as it cooked, with browned flour sprinkled in the fat sizzling under the head. She strewed on thyme and sage and bay. And when she brought the head to table, grinning beatifically with its crackling lips and puffed jowls, there were two red cranberries for eyes and a lemon in the mouth, to give a touch of contrasting color and extra fillip to the taste. We felt like mediaeval barons and baronesses in their high Norman halls.

Caput apri refero
Resonans laudes Domino!

Did you ever bite into a roast-pig's ear? If not, then there is a passionate experience still coming to you. The resistance to the teeth provided by the cartilage lining in that part of the pig which listens for the slop of the gruel in the evening's bucket is something that cannot be described, but it is great joy in a tangible form.

But there's another as delectable way of eating the pig's headpiece. And several of our November pigs always lost their heads in this cold and captivating dish, so utterly different from the taste of roast boar. This was hog's-head-cheese. It was one of the traditional Maine marriages of different textures and flavors in meat that have made Maine people easily able to come smiling through the coldest and hardest of weathers. It is tidbits of marrow suspended in a jelly of the gods. It is stout biting and melting magic, with sharp sage and other savory herbs suffusing it through and through. You put it away in pans in pantries like heirlooms. You come upon it late at night, when you had thought it had all been eaten months ago, you slice off slabs of it and eat it by pounds and pounds and go to bed and dream of your grandmother—but of the pleasant one of your two!

To start the cheese off, you cut off the pig's ears, dig out his eyes. Then you stew the head, and the cleaned ears, in a thick iron kettle, in salted water, till the meat begins to fall from the bone. Save the stock. Take all the meat off the bones and run it through your wooden chopping-tray. Stir sage and a chopped, raw onion into the meat-stock. Put your chopped meat back in. Let the whole mess boil a few minutes more. Last, pour the whole business into a shallow crock and set it high on the pantry shelf where Uncle Asas cannot find it, and let it cool. Set it outdoors if Uncle Asa isn't around. The liquid solidifies as it cools. The gelatinous substance cooked out of the bones in the stock holds all the variegated tidbits of ear and jowl and cheek and cartilage suspended in a firm jelly. You can slice it with a knife.

Our November meant going from one promontory of pleasure to another. From the North Pole of our pig we leapt to the South. After we had eaten the head roasted or cheesed, we went for the feet. Pigs' trotters, we called them. And we served them up in several ways also. But I think pigs' feet with dumplings was tops.

My mother washed the feet and cut off the toe-nails. Then she cooked them slowly in her big pioneer iron kettle. When they grew tender and pneumatic to the fork, she salted them to taste. Then when the meat was about done, she put in sliced onions—two or three of them. The dumplings were the crown to the dish. She mixed one teaspoon of salt into two cups of sifted flour, added just water enough so she could roll the flour out like piecrust on her floured breadboard. Then she cut the dumplings into resilient rectangles, sloshed each one back and forth with her hand in the stew, and dropped it in, to become transfigured and explode into a marvel. When one was well on its way, she put in the next. Sometimes, for a change, she made dough-devils—raised dumplings, that is—instead of the educated rolled kind. She made them always for Uncle Asa, as they had more bulk and filled up faster. There was a righteous lot to Uncle Asa to fill. He was the kind of man who might conceal a whole pig in his pants! Whatever dumplings mother made, she gave them fifteen sweet moments in the broth, with the cover set on tight.

Pigs' feet, like pigs' heads, are full of magic. There's a kind of texture in them found in no other meat. They are velvet and silk and plush among the meats. When you bite them, their resistance makes a wolf of you, you bolt them and do not know how to stop. The flavor is a cross between marrow and honey. The dumplings add still another delight with their flavor of transfigured cereal. Men will founder on a kettle of pigs' feet if a woman is not around to hold them back after the fifth plate.

Naturally our farm pigs had fine fifteen-pound hams and bacon that held the flavor of acorns and beechnuts we gathered for them in our own forests. Naturally they filled barrels with their fine white belly-rinds of salted pork. We had sausage meat, too. But these are the staples that tide a family through a Winter. The cream of our crop we ate at the time of the pig-sticking and the season of last squeals. Heads and feet, hearts and liver and delicate, perishable spare-ribs—these were our jewels. They made November the sweetest month of the year at the table.

I like to paint the portrait of a happy man. He is the man who sits in his house while the gray sky is spitting its first snow. There is a smile all over the man's face. For there is a pig cut wide open to the world in his woodshed. There are sausages in garlands strung all around the pantry. A barrel of newly salted pork is right under the man's broad foundations, in his cellar. Hams are darkening and sweetening in his dark and sooty chimney. The man leans back in glory. For under his ribs are about a dozen spare-ribs. Before them, there had been a dozen crescents of fresh liver. That man will never mind taxes or Uncle Asas or wars. Whatever comes, he will take all like a philosopher. For he has had his hours of bliss, sitting outside his own spare-ribs. He has ripened with his fat pigs at the ripe end of the year!

19. Down-East Breakfast

WEATHER, mother of good poetry, is also mother of good breakfasts. The solider the weather, the solider the meal. The sharper the air, the sharper the appetite. Maine runs to fine breakfasts as it runs to fine poetry. The world's biggest breakfast, which was the oldtime Maine farm-meal of the morning, could never have originated and developed south of the halfway mark from the Equator to the North

Pole. It took a lot of hardy subarctic cold and sting and bite to the air to bring out its very substantial contours.

Like the American "tea" of a century ago, which faded out into our modern supper, the American farm-breakfast of the north was a whole three-ring meal, maybe one of the only two meals a man was going to get; and so it was built with strong buttresses, to buttress him about for a hard day's work, in the sprucewoods, on the Fundy swells, in snow up to his middle, in no'theasters and sou'westers he had to lean on to keep standing.

Unless a man had a lot of ballast at his middle, he might never go through the day and come home to his loved ones at sundown. The few oldtimers who, for dyspepsia or love or other reasons, ate light in the morning, never came home from a heavy spell of weather to beget their kind. They blew away. The heavy-breakfasters begot heavy heirs, and they stayed put.

It was a pioneer meal, that ancient breakfast, a meal for men who were carving a nation out of forests and earth and mountains. It was a prelude to the two-bladed axe, the cant-dog, the crowbar, the scythe, or the adze. It was the only proper breakfast for the man with fists like mauls and thighs like young oak trees.

It still is, in Maine. The present-day Maine outdoors man is built on the same solid foundations as his pioneer grandfather, and he sticks close to his cordwood or his lobster traps because he is hefted down to stay with several pounds of solid breakfast. Our best citizens are still mostly farmers and fisher-men, outdoors men, and the standard Maine breakfast is cut even now to fit such men's jobs. It cannot be a pindling, an indoors sort of thing. The Maine man has to do his day's work in weather like the edge on a crosscut saw, like a breeze in Baffin Land, like an Old-Home Week among the icebergs. So he better eat hearty, or he won't last the day's weather out.

The Maine morning meal is like a tune on the bag-pipes which calls the stout-hearted Scot to war. It is something that must strengthen him deep to his marrow, and only the mas-culine and downright victuals will do. The ordinary Ameri-can breakfast, with its precooked and predigested cereals, its humming-bird nectar of citrus, butterflies of bacon, and aenemias of eggs is as much out of place in Maine as a sarong, as a French breakfast of a dry roll and *chocolat-chaud* would be to an Eskimo of Greenland. It would be an insult to his oily manhood. Fat is the foe of weather, and fat is the making of Maine's first meal.

The *habitant* breakfast of the Province of Quebec is a brawny brother to the Maine one. Good reason why; it is a doughnut bronzed in the same fat. The French-Canadian has ten-twelve hours of work ahead of him, out in the blue blazes of Winter sun, weather, and water, and it behooves him to put a hefty, hot, bronzed breakfast under his belt if he is go-ing to stand up to the tough logs and tough codfish of the day's job.

[232]

The basic principle of this northern North American, Laurentian, or Kennebecan breakfast is that it must stick by the ribs a long time. It must stay put and generate heat. It must be food that takes a long time to get digested, that keeps, to quote a Maine man, "a-nourishing and a-nourishing ye for nine-ten hours." It must have rich, fattened and oiled doughnuts to it, heavy pies and pancakes, to keep the stomach busy, to keep the blood away from a man's brain, where it can only do mischief, to keep his blood in his arms and thighs where a good woodchopper's or smelt-fisherman's blood belongs. It should have bulk enough to keep the inner man busy for ten-twelve hours, say. For few farmers or fishermen I know would ever dream of coming home at midday. It would be like telling stories in haying-time, making love in a dance-hall. It would be like walking out on the job; it would be like a strong man putting on skirts.

The Maine breakfast is a hefty meal for hefty he-men.

The Down-East breakfast is concocted under the sign of the frying pan. Hot fat is at its heart. It begins with a seething and bubbling of pork fat in the skillet or spider. Fat salt pork in chunks, not lean and feminine bacon rashers, is its base.

The flapjack is the wrapper to all the solid foods the working man gets outside of, once he gets inside his pants, starts weathering up against the weather, and begins the day's work by working four-five pounds of flour, fat, meat, and pie into him as his first job. For this breakfast *is* a job, and only the brawny can bring it off with a flourish. And the flapjack is a rather solid wrapper to wrap all this substance in.

The Down-East farm-flapjack is the outdoors, masculine, New World *crêpe-suzette*. It is about as much like its relative in Paris, in London, or in our own sunny South, as an all-American tackle is like a boy in pants six inches long playing with a ten-cent-store football. It is the same fruit, but grown up and with great strength upon it. It is just the size of the whole spider it is cooked in.

The flapjack cook gives her creation the works. She uses no prepared and effete pancake-mix. She uses plain buck-wheat or wheat flour, sour milk, salt, two even teaspoons of cream-o'-tartar, one of saleratus, a tablespoon of sugar, elbow grease, a tablespoon of shortening, a large duck's egg, and vigor, to mix it up. She pours it out of a gallon pitcher into an old-fashioned, thick-iron frying pan, sending up volcanoes of blue smoke from its sizzling pork fat, and she fills the spider full of her dough from rim to rim. She sears her dough-flap brown on its port side, as she can tell when it begins to bubble over all its continental width, tosses it high into the air, big as the frying pan itself, catches it exquisitely as it comes hurtling down, on the horizontal, without smear-ing the rim of her pan, catches it squarely on its starboard, sears it, this side, to a light mahogany, and tosses it table-wards to her hungering man. The parade of flying flapjacks is continuous. The good cook keeps the kitchen air full of them, being flapped over the fat or over to the table.

These flapjacks are a steady procession of wrappings for the more substantial victuals the man is stowing away meantime. The man wraps up each cod-steak or pork-chop or beefsteak in one of these hot blankets of dough as he downs it. A good man can get outside of six or seven of these fringes or wrappers to his real breakfast victuals.

These main dishes of Maine are of many solid kinds. But all are hefty. The ideal breakfast will include three or four or five of them.

Here is a list of the more pronounced ones of the lot. Hulled corn (hominy to the less husky eaters of Wisconsin and Minnesota) washed down cold in thick hot molasses is a pretty fair dish. Cold pigs' feet standing up in the jelly of the cooled broth they were cooked in are always in good taste. A beefsteak, thick and wide enough to fill up the spider from side to side, fried till it is charred almost black on the outside and gets light brown only after you get two inches in—that is a dish always current. Or a man might hanker for a little of last night's corn-meal mush, and his wife will slice a big bowlful of it into thick slabs and sear it brown in her frying pan, and he will eat the slabs with a pint of red-hot maple syrup from his own maples up back of the henhouse.

A man may choose between the hulled corn and the mush, and take only the steak and pass the pigs'-feet-in-jelly by. But

[235]

he will probably take the two kinds of fish. Smothered eels and fried cod-steaks, both. The basis of both is pork. The eels are stewed slow in a thickened pork-gravy. The cod is fried with hunks of pork the size of a man's thumb so crisp that they melt away in the mouth. The man eats maybe a sixth of a pound of pork along with his well-browned cod and his hot jellied eels without conscious effort, without noticing anything but the flavor of it. It is easy eating.

In any case, there must be the cheese. And when I say cheese, I don't mean something that starts out as a mollycoddle of a food for babies like milk. I mean cheese with meat to it. A solid phalanx of fat, lean, gristle, embedded in a firm delectable jelly the meats themselves have made. I mean calves'-head cheese or pig's-head cheese. I mean meat. I mean the meat that has been boiled off a calf's head or a pig's, till the skull bones are bare and taken out, the meat chopped fine with a chopper, sage and bayberry sprinkled in, salted and peppered, poured back into the broth, and the whole business left to settle and grow wise. As it cools, the dish composes itself into a massy continent which has to be cut with the butcher knife. This is strenuous and fine eating, and it makes a "stick-by-the-ribs-Billy" dish that will take a man straight through three cords of beechwood or the whole length of a string of a hundred lobster traps without a rest and with a song in the mouth.

The hog's-head cheese of Maine is one of this unhappy world's happiest dishes. It contains the jowls and muscles, those delicious pockets of lean along the brows, the half-fat, half-lean tissues over the cheek bones, the half-marrow, half-heaven of the juices inside the porous head bones, the toothsome tough fabric of the resilient skin-rind. It is jellied in its own savory jelly.

Of course, the pig's head frightens most people away from its nectarean hulk. But the tastiest part of your pig is his head, as it is with the cod. The Maine farmer alone has kept this meat for kings, the boar's head, still on the democratic table, to the delight and strength of men.

One of the secrets of this dish—which I ought to be ostracized for letting out of the bag this way to the other states west and south—is the deer meat in it. For the wise Maine wife chops in with the pig's meat strings from the deer hung in the woodshed, and this lean wild venison points up the tame gelatinous pig meat till it tastes exactly as lusty and intoxicating as the meat of the wild boar of the Middle Ages.

Naturally—and this breakfast is all nature and good-natured eating—there is a liquid being constantly drunk to float all these ships of heavy meats and fish and wheat or buckwheat on. It is tea. It is scalding hot tea that fills the farmer's eyes with unsorrowful tears till they drip from his moustache or chin. It is the color of Javanese mahogany. It is as black as your hat. It is about as near to the tea drunk at tea parties by women and womanish men as the male in three-cornered pants is to the adult one in overalls that can stand by themselves. The spoon can nearly stand in this tea. This brew has been steeping in a teapot the size of the teakettle. It has been boiled right up and down for lo these many days. It comes from the teapot that steams forever on the back of the Maine stove, in season and out, replenished and freshened with fistfuls of fresh tea leaves every other day or so.

Five cupfuls of this liquid iron, of this red-hot brew is the minimum to float the average breakfast. Some of the older men a bit past their full bloom, or some younger ones not yet come to theirs and having peach-fuzz instead of whiskers on their cheeks, dilute this tea with sugar and milk. But the middle and powerful males take its tannin into themselves neat. It galvanizes their "innerds," they say, against the damp and cold. *Yerba maté!* Hunh! It is pink lemonade beside this whisky of the north that keeps the lumberjack and the lobsterman going strong.

"Fat pork and strong tea." That is the Maine proverb for a good standard breakfast. Another wise saying is that tea is tea only when it puts whiskers on the soles of your feet. Maine men's feet have hair on their bottoms so they can cling to their dories and rolling logs.

And so, solidly, we come to dessert. For dessert this one of the two substantial meals of the Maine day must have. Sugar is a fuel for the working man, and it cannot be left out of his morning menu. Of course, he has already got some sweetness into himself in the honey, maple sugar, or molasses he has had on his cornmeal and flapjacks. But that was merely an accompaniment of sweetness. He must take it pure and unadulterated at the close of his breakfast.

So the wise woman of the house trots out her pies, hot and cold, custard, cream, cranberry, mince, apple, cherry, squash, punkin, blueberry, huckleberry, lemon, or vinegar. Maybe four or five of this lot if she has them. And the smart wife usually does have at least three kinds on her pantry shelves. A man that is a man can generally take care of four-five pieces of pie. And a piece of pie, in Maine, means usually a quarter, for most housewives cut but two diameters when they take a pie apart.

And when the man lets out his belt at last to the last notch, brushes the piecrust off his vest, and gets up to get going at his saw, his axe, his gas engine, or his plow, he goes out of his home with the wifely kiss on his lips, and her blessing for the day, with two hands of doughnuts. That is, he has a doughnut, from the four-gallon stone crock which is always within arm's length of the breakfast table, on each one of the fingers on his two hands.

"Eiah," as a Maine man says when he is feeling in the affirmative, the Maine breakfast is the keystone, the cornerstone of the whole day's work. It is the first and biggest meal. It is a symphony concert of the North, the proper prelude to manhood, a three-ring circus of dough, of meat, of sweet, of fat. It is a square dance of a square meal, *up and down the center, all promenade, and eight hands around!*

V

THE STATE OF
MAINE

20. Cradle of Democracy

THE cradle is the best piece of furniture in a house. Empty or full, it is the family's heart. But a cradle that is full is a sure sign the family is going to endure.

In New England we have a cradle that is still full. It is an old cradle—older than any of the nations as we know them now, except China, possibly. Possibly it is older than China, even. For this cradle of ours which is still busy rocked in the forests and fogs of ancient Germany and Scandinavia long before the Child Who Changed the Shape of the World lay in swaddling clothes on the straw of the Bethlehem stable.

Our cradle is the New England town meeting. It began rocking ages ago when the bearded men of the Angles and Saxons and Jutes sat down to straighten themselves out and settle their affairs for a whole year at one sitting. The cradle went on rocking overseas in England, and it was the core of Alfred the Great's Kingdom of Wessex. It rocked on into the broad foundations of the great England that emerged from the Middle Ages. A meeting of men who governed themselves, common men working out justice in common—that was the germ and seed of the modern world-principle called democracy.

The cradle came over the Atlantic in the *Mayflower*. It rocked in the woods of Plymouth and Boston. It rocked away west over all New England, wherever three or four houses clung together in a clearing in the continental woods. And it rocked away west out of New England, across the Hudson, over the Appalachians, the prairies, and the Rocky Mountains, till it came to the Pacific's shore. And now it springs up in the Philippines, on its way to complete its circumnavigation of the globe.

Out of our cradle came the Minute Man, the Continental Congress, the *Declaration of Independence,* and the *Constitution.* Out of it came also the flame that burned backwards

[244]

over the sea and set France on fire, and spread out over Europe in the nineteenth century as the dream of the shape of things to come.

But here in New England we still have that shape of democracy in its pure, young, and lusty form. The baby of democracy is still in our midst, kicking off the clothes and using his lungs at their loudest. Every New England town that is still small enough to crowd into one big hall crowds in there once a year, and fixes up its schools, its streets and roads, and its finances at one lively sitting, does all its business, and then sits down to apple pie and doughnuts and a good time. Ancient English towns, Durham and Topsham, Yarmouth and Ipswich, Barnstable and Bridgton, are at home in a new land, with the same names on them and the same meetings of the townsfolk going on at full cry.

It wasn't chance, it was divinity that saw to it that our forefathers hit upon the month of March as town-meeting time. The world, the ancients believed, began in March. In March the snake sheds his skin. The year in the North really does begin then, and so town meeting comes in mud-time, before plowing, when the frost is going out of the world and mayflowers and young frogs are coming in. So it is the right time for a town to come out, make the world over, renew its skin like the snake, its youth like the eagle, and come forth revigorated, refinanced, and resplendent.

And the whole town does come out. Not just the men—men, women, children, and babes in arms. For our institution of town meeting has not stood still. It has kept up with the times. Our women vote, our children take part. Our cradle takes in the whole community. It is an improvement on the old male Anglo-Saxon crib! It is good to begin governing yourself young. And we do. Many a citizen of us raises his voice in town affairs when he is still in trousers that are held up by a safety-pin.

Town meeting is a family affair. It is Old Home Week and family reunions, as well as school budgets and appropriations for roads and street lamps. The women swop recipes for upside-down-cake, and the farmers swop ideas on fertilizer and feed. It is not all voting and debate. It is the beginnings of courtships, too, and visits of friends who have not seen one another all through the deep snows of Winter. Improved mince pies, as well as better lighting and school books and better cows and potatoes, come out of this gathering of the town fathers and mothers and children. Conviviality and friendship mean as much to a community as good laws, and this is the town visiting day when such vital things flower.

The town's business is, of course, the core of the day. And it is all done up for the year on this first Monday in March. The elections come first. The voters choose their Selectmen, their School Board, the Commissioner of Highways, and Collector of Taxes. This voting is by ballot, in the forenoon. Then lunchboxes come out, the families gather around them, warming up the benches they are to burgeon on in the afternoon. But it is the afternoon that sees the government of the people, for the people, by the people in full swing. After the Moderator—who must be a cross between King Solomon and St. Francis of Assisi—has been elected and takes his place with his gavel, the town sits back on its skirts and trousers and its wits and ideas of fair play and civic sense, and man after woman stands and orates and argues and votes the town's way through maybe seventy-nine or eighty-seven articles in the town warrant. That warrant has been worked up by a committee to whom the citizens have sent lists of their grievances and ideas, and it has been posted for some days in public. Now each voter has a copy of it in his hands. It covers every item of civic weal, from a new culvert on the River Road, costing $7.50, to the appropriation for the support of the free public schools, amounting to maybe $25,000.00. Fire protection, repair of roads, maintenance of the poor, and flags and pencils for school children are some of the items which strike out the most sparks.

Sparks are struck out and fill the room with fire. It isn't the size of the expenditure proposed that kindles the fire. It's the principle. And small-town people are great on principle. Village Hampdens and cornfield Websters rise up and burst into oratory. There is no limit set on speech; speech is free, and everybody says his say. These small town Ciceros essay questions of morals and *mores* great Cicero would have trembled to approach. Encouraged by his neighbors' cheers, or his wife, a plain farmer with weather on his face or a plumber with rust on his hands becomes a tower of civic righteousness and changes the shape of his town's history. The voting is by a show of hands. The larger number of hands carries the day. In close votes, the hands are painstakingly counted one by one by tellers who perambulate the hall. It all takes time. The March sun sets, and all the ways grow dark. Oratory still flames. But it is worth the time and pains. For good citizens are being made this day, and a long day is none too long for that business. Good citizens are what the world needs most in these dark times. They will have plenty to do.

All the town's problems are settled here in the town hall. Not in Washington. The Federal government is something far away and unreal, save when the long hand of war comes and touches men's clothes and turns them into khaki or blue. The State Capital is distant, too, and it touches only the township's roads and automobiles. The County Seat is a shadowy thing also save in suits of law. The New England town is its own law-maker and governor. It is a small universe by itself. And in this small universe men and women move resourcefully and independently from their cradles to their graves.

Independence is the word. Each tub stands on its own bottom. The majority rules, but the minority always makes itself heard and is respected. Of course this form of government means delays and lost motions and discouragements in civic progress. But it pays richly in the long run. The God-given right every Yankee enjoys of disagreeing with everybody and everything still keeps alive. Men take pride in being against the majority, against the government, against everything in the universe but the law of being a good neighbor and trying to follow the Golden Rule. Yankee crankiness may put trigs to the wheels of progress, cut down appropriations for worthy causes, but it is a crankiness such as that which built the slow British Commonwealth, the experiment called the United States of America, and such as will keep dictators out of the world tomorrow. The right to disagree is a divine right, and it still lifts a lusty voice in this ancient cradle of the New England town meeting, this cradle which will help breed good citizens for a world set free in the years to come.

More likely than not, the town meeting, begun with the minister's invocation of God, winds up with a dinner of a dozen breeds of New England pies and layer-cake and baked beans. And the rulers of themselves sit down hearty, having settled their schools and roads and morals for one more year, and eat their way right down through the whole culinary foundation of New England virtue!

It is a pretty old religion, this Anglo-Saxon religion of self-government. But it is still alive in the world. And the world ought to be thankful for it.

21. Maine: State of Being Oneself

THE State of Maine has a rugged face towards the Atlantic. It has high cheek bones, shaggy eyebrows, and a prominent chin, being all mountains, woods, and deep bays. On the map it looks gaunt. But gauntness is a good old American habit in faces. Rugged faces look good outdoors and in the weather. Maine looks very good in the weather and light. It has a lot of both. And the State of Maine gets the sun on its face first of all these United States.

My state wakes up first and wakes all America up. It is the rooster that calls us Americans to the favorite American sport, hard work. Maine people do a lot of hard work. But you seldom hear about it. It is so natural, so taken for granted, so much like play.

Dirigo. "I lead." But Maine's motto is modestly confined to geography. It does not claim leadership in economics, culture, crime, or anything else. Moderation is almost our only unbroken state law. Our best people are moderates—"mod'rits," as they say it, saving their breath for the oars and the bucksaw. They have aspired to lead the nation in nothing save staying American according to the older rural and village patterns, and preceding the United States, or Vermont, in going Republican in Presidential elections.

Older than Massachusetts in its first settlement, deeply New England in its virtues and vices, houses, barns, thrift, and sharp-cornered individualism, Maine figures less than any of the other New England states in national publicity and in the history textbooks. It is the state of *litotes,* understatement, reticences, and mistrust of bandwagons, loud-speakers, and campaigns for establishing righteousness by acts of legislature. Most of our adages are ones calculated to caution people, to take the wind out of big sails—our own included—and to look at a horse at both ends. We have been slower than other states at buying gold bricks, subscribing to new deals, or improving our neighbors' morals. We have had quite enough to do keeping our own morals ship-shape and up to scratch.

No wonder the British historian Toynbee sets us down as not having done so much as Massachusetts towards our national culture. We are a "museum piece—a relic of seventeenth-century New England inhabited by woodmen and watermen and hunters. . . . Maine today is at once one of the longest-settled regions of the North American Union and one of the least urbanized and sophisticated." Arnold Toynbee blames it all on the weather. It has been too much for us. "How is this contrast between Maine and Massachusetts to be explained? It would appear that the hardness of the New England environment, which stands at its optimum in Massachusetts, is accentuated in Maine to a degree at which it brings in diminishing returns of human response."

To look at us, or to hear us talk, you might think Toynbee is right. Lord knows our climate and soil are hard enough and cold enough to keep anybody busy just barely keeping alive. Maine cows run thin; they have hard work getting enough to eat between junipers and ledges. Our farmers live, mostly, on one-horse farms, where a tractor would break its back.

Yet Toynbee, like so many historians, Americans among them, who count noses and statistics and state papers, is wrong. Historians who stick to acts of assembly, wars, state and institutional archives often do miss the intangibles that mean more to culture than any programs of civic enlargement.

It is true that Maine has never got much into the history

books. We did not run true to the Puritan ecclesiastical pattern from our beginnings. So, when all history was church history, we got left out in the cold. The first New England church was an Anglican one, at the Kennebec's mouth, 1608. We had some good early settlers, but they weren't always of the right politics. Some of our first families did not leave calling-cards; they were no better than they should be—often not even that! They left their European home towns without leaving a forwarding address. They came over here for good reasons, but not the going churchly ones. Hence historians overlook the fact that the model for all later American commonwealths founded on the principles of religious toleration and of minority rights is Sir Ferdinando Gorges' colonial experiment in Maine. It was too free for Puritan Massachusetts, and so it died a sudden death when Charles the First was beheaded. The first graveyard with Roman Catholics and Protestants buried side by side is on an island off Maine.

Most of our Maine history is marginal. There are no good records kept of it, no archives of deeds and charters. It supplements Massachusetts or America at large. A good deal of our civic strength has been used up in minding our own business and letting other people alone. Yet when the nation needed our aid, it was usually there. In the French and Indian wars, Maine men cracked the Gibraltar of the western hemisphere at Louisburg. But Maine history was Massachusetts history then. In the Revolution, Maine furnished as many men in proportion to its population as Massachusetts.

In proportion to its population Maine was the most maritime of all the states when American history, between 1815 and 1880, was being written on the seas of the globe. In the Civil War, Maine led all the Union states in per capita attendance on that fight for survival. It was hardest hit of all northern states. One in every five males in Portland was in uniform. Whole towns disappeared. The President of Bowdoin College took the college *en masse* to war. In the last two global wars, Maine men fought in as high a proportion as any state on land, on sea, in the air. But we were so small we had no regiments or divisions with our Pine Tree emblem.

Maine's population, not much larger now than in 1860, is about that of Cleveland, Ohio. The statistics are always bound to be against us, therefore. At any moment, we seem to be small potatoes and few in a hill. But we do raise potatoes. And it is partly our fault that our achievements escape Mr. Toynbee. We have never gone in for historical monuments or for societies for the preservation or publicizing of antiquities or civic righteousnesses. We have been more interested in making the present chimney draw, digging today's mess of clams, or giving our children a good education than in advertising our ancestors. We have trusted in monuments too little and in little boys and girls too much to bulk large historically.

But we have got along pretty well without getting into the history books. History books have a way of going out of date and gathering dust; and men who work hard and mind their own business, make their own boats and lobster traps, have a way of outlasting the statistics and contributing to the national life even if unmentioned in the newspapers.

A lot of Maine history is in forms Mr. Toynbee and other historians have no yardstick to measure. For instance, Maine's history is in Ohio, Indiana, Illinois, Michigan, Wisconsin, Minnesota, Oregon, and Washington. Maine helped many states to get on their feet and make a good start. Every third or so of the pioneer families in those states hailed from Maine. Maine lumbermen, farmers, humorists (we have had to breed them or die!), dairymen, boat-builders, engineers and men of gadgets have been, for one hundred and fifty years, the standard for all America. Other states feathered their nests out of Maine's cold little nest.

The chief history of Maine is an elegy. Our leading export has been, save for the century of wooden ships, our smartest children. So the railroads across the continent, the shipyards of California, the farms of Nebraska, Kansas, Oklahoma, and even Texas, and the mines of the Rockies are good Maine history. Except when we enlarged the front-dooryards to our farms and gave our boys Java and the Horn and China to play with, we did not have enough work to keep our most ambitious children at home. So Maine became a seed-bed for the United States at large.

I am constantly amazed, as I go reading my poems over our country, to discover that a good part of my audiences, in whatever state I read, have ancestors in Maine. Maine

[255]

might be called a state of good ancestors. It is a way of assuring oneself of forebears who believed in hard, independent American work to pick them up in Maine. Many Americans do. Too bad such facts cannot get into tables of statistics for Mr. Toynbee to read!

What we have in Maine is the sort of thing that can get into literature and art, though. It always has been so in art. Leave the bright light and lace-like evergreens and rocks of Maine out of American art, and you will leave a big hole. Most American artists, from Homer on, have come Down East to see men and skies and waves and cliffs at their cleanest and handsomest best.

We have been a bit slower in making our mark on literature. Of course, we produced the creator of the Rollo books and Kellogg of the score of boyhood classics a century ago. And Longfellow was Maine, and Hawthorne, at least part time. Sarah Orne Jewett was the first of our modern American realists. Frost and Wilder have sense enough to have ancestors in Maine. One of the two greatest American poets of the century, Edwin Arlington Robinson, hailed from "Tilbury Town," Gardiner on the Kennebec. And, of course, Edna St. Vincent Millay, best woman poet this side of Sappho, is a Maine girl, hailing from Rockland. "Renascence," wake-up poem of the twentieth century, blossomed out on Penobscot Bay. Today, too, there are Mary Ellen Chase, Gladys Hasty Carroll, Kenneth Roberts, Wilbert Snow, Ruth Moore, Elisabeth Ogilvie, Henry Beston, Elizabeth Coatsworth, Elinor Graham, and a host of other poets and novelists putting Maine on the literary map. Too bad Mr. Toynbee's historical tables cannot take into account such lights that can make a state sparkle in the eyes of a whole world. But, as I said before, history cannot measure light.

The secret of these writers is the strength in the modern theme of local color. If you get down to bedrock in one state, you get down to bedrock in all states and all nations. The realism of today's prose and poetry is a realism of fundamental humanity. Maine is a fine hunting ground for humanity because the older and more enduring designs in human nature are still here, in this piscatorial and agricultural land: humor, folk speech, stories, proverbs, and occupational techniques of work by hand and heart that spell something close to wisdom itself and add up to civilization.

Here I go, breaking the one unbreakable Maine law of understatement. But a poet of Maine has to because his people will not. He has to be the lyrical outlet of their silent and natural lyricism. For years I have laid myself open to being called a rhapsodist of Maine. I cannot help being such, being a poet.

The thing of it is, Maine had always been so naturally a lyric poem, in hard weather and times especially, despite Mr. Toynbee, that we did not have to produce writers and poets. Our people were naturally such, going about their varied and exciting work so akin to play, being themselves without books of rules. Only lately have we begun to write our life down for outsiders' enjoyment. Maybe Mr. Toynbee doesn't read poems and novels. Many historians don't have time to, reading so many so-called vital statistics as they do.

Thoreau, a Massachusetts man, did not find us, as Toynbee does, unsophisticated. "The deeper you penetrate into the woods, the more intelligent and, in one sense, less countrified do you find the inhabitants." But Thoreau was a philosopher and did not pay his taxes!

Naturally we have our sins and our share of skeletons in the closet. If they do not bulk so large as the crookednesses in some states, maybe it is our size that saves us. Even our sins do not make the front page.

Let's see: we fathered Neal Dow, father of prohibition. But many sincere people count him as a saint and not a sinner. Once, very briefly, the Klan reared its ugly hooded head, but that is down now. We are said to be snobbish and standoffish to Summer people. We had reason to be when they patronized us or looked down their noses at us and called us "natives." Today we are different, and they are, too. They want to belong and be neighbors, and, though we are cautious and slow at making friends, we make them for keeps. Our million Summer people now are our friends.

Other, deeper sins we have. We have allowed our "white coal"—Maine has limitless water-power—to get into the hands of monopolists at times. Worse still, we have let the mills at all our waterfalls poison our rivers with chemicals and kill out all our famous salmon and shad. That pollution still goes on and makes a desert of some of the best rivers of America. We have slaughtered our forests, left the slash, and let forest fires burn up our soil and the substance of children to come. Here is our blackest sin. Unintelligence and greed are as common in Maine as elsewhere. I think what the lumber interests and pulp interests have done to the forest which was Maine deserves to rank as a capital crime. Some counties are deserts now. Our firs along our coast are being butchered for the comics. As I write this, a dozen forest fires are eating up our soil and our future around me. We could have made Maine another Norway if we had farmed our forests intelligently. We may do it even yet. For in spite of our greed and shortsightedness, new balsams and pines keep coming up. Maine evergreens are hard to kill. We have always been able to raise a new crop.

Oh, we have had crops Mr. Toynbee or somebody in the field of economics could have measured. At any given time, in proportion to our population—always remembering the size of Cleveland—we have turned out a powerful lot of things.

First it was ships. We covered the globe with them. Maine sails whitened the Mediterranean and South Pacific. Maine babies got themselves born off Good Hope and cut their teeth off the peaks of Java. Every Maine one-horse farmer had vast sailing vessels working for him. That was a time, our golden hundred years Mr. Toynbee should have found statistics on somewhere, when a small Maine coast town like my own bred two hundred sea captains, and some of its families built, and sailed, in three generations, over seventy ships apiece. That was a time when Maine citizens had great friendships in Liverpool, Batavia, Valparaiso, Rio, and Bremen; when all the oceans were crowded with peaceful traders of all nations and we were much closer to the One World Wendell Willkie dreamed of than we are now. Maine bulked large then in global history and international commonwealths of sail. Maine barns had Chinese temples for their cupolas, and our ships of oak and pine were the world's standard.

Then we had lumber. The Kennebec and Penobscot overran with logs; our trees traveled to the earth's ends. Maine produced Paul Bunyan and sent him off singing to log off Wisconsin, Michigan, and Washington State. Probably Mr. Toynbee never heard of him. He is almost as important, in culture, as his remote cousin, John Bunyan!

After logs, it was ice. Kennebec ice cooled India and the Argentine. The icehouses along the river were like cathedrals and shook with the music of strong men working with cant-dogs and ice-picks, storing diamonds of Maine Winters to keep the earth fresh and cool.

Our Kennebec salmon once were standard. So were, and are still, our herring, cod, lobsters. Our lobsters go now by airplane to all the country. We make a lot of Yankee notions still, gadgets of wood and metal. At Bath, we built destroyers at the rate of two or so a month for the United States Navy.

Whatever Yankee ingenuity demands, be it clothespins, shoes, or skis or canoes, we still turn them out.

We raise a lot of potatoes. Aroostook, one county the size of most New England states, raises fifteen per cent, up to eighty million bushels, of the world's potatoes. But we raise a varied crop, too—smaller potatoes, cows, hens, apples, home-made reach-boats and dories and lobster traps, which make us our living and the living for over a million Summer residents, on our small farms along our twenty-five hundred miles of coast and among our forests and lakes.

The most thriving industry at the moment is the Summer tourists. These we tan and send home, from children's camps and beaches and hotels, to the rest of the United States, rejoicing. And we provide a lot of Americans with camping and fishing and hunting, old American pioneer occupations, in season. Seventy-five thousand deer go out of the state each Fall on automobiles.

But these are all crops that, like our wooden ships of the past, can evaporate and disappear. We have much more lasting harvests than all such. We have never measured our best things by the barrel, the bushel, or the pound. There are our intangibles that only philosophy and art and poetry can preserve and perpetuate, that do not go out of existence ever, that add up to what Maine really is.

Call the roll:

First, Maine is not so much a state as a state of weather and scenery. We have a seacoast like a continuous Rio de Janeiro.

Our mountains and woods come down to the sea and crowd out on the islands and ocean. Our farms are fog-horns and lighthouses and silver hordes of smelts and herring and thundering horsefish, as well as barns and plows and freckled-faced boys. Our winds blow out of the *Book of Revelation*. We go bent to suit the gales. Days we have like glass in a Sandwich plate. Northern Lights and blazing stars light us in the cold half of the year. Our ten thousand islands are citadels of loveliness and loneliness and teach us the art of making our own way in life. Our wiry children are cousins of the bobcat and deer. We have as much sunshine in Winter as Summer; we are greener in our snow months than in our leaf months, thanks to our evergreens. Weather and beauty can add up to a culture faster than battles and charters. Toynbee ought to be told this. These are our jewels.

Next, Maine is not so much a state as a state of mind. It is the live-and-let-live philosophy of living with your neighbor without trying too hard to improve him. For the group coercions of modern mass-society—be it fascism or communism—Maine has a hate that amounts to an obsession. It shows in our politics, in our unwillingness to join crusades. It appears in Maine people's way of looking at things squarely and taking time to make up their mind; it appears in charity, which is the art of not being better than your neighbor. Maine caution can be the beginning of wisdom. It can flower in integrity. I know lobstermen who look more like Marcus Aurelius and Abraham Lincoln than most of our politicians

do. Odd—or natural, rather!—that one should look for states-
manly faces among boat-builders and farmers.

Maine is still a state of thrift. Men and women still believe
in saving up against storms and old age. It is not reprehen-
sible here for men to take care for their own futures and not
expect the state to do it. Hard work is still so respected that
most of our working people, including myself, refuse to
abide by an eight-hour day. The best work, as the best poem,
is an overtime affair, done when other people sleep, in low-
ebb hours, by starlight, by lantern light.

It is the Maine people, after all, that mean what Maine
means most. The people haven't amassed great wealth or cut
wide swaths in politics; but they have learned how to get
along on small but hardy apples, little berries, small boats,
the shellfish and lobsters they wrest from the sea. They have
rocky acres, a few cows, two months free of frost, blows you
can hitch a horse to, rough waters, wild and hungry and
lonely stretches of forest and sea; yet they make both ends
meet, get along with their own minds, and grow into men
who look well in oil paintings and bronze.

These people are the most all-round Americans we have
left. They are farmers or fishermen or small-town working
men; yet they send sons and daughters to college and into the
professions. They are hunters, too, have libraries, keep posted
on history and politics. They have refrigerators and electric
stoves and radios, but they do a lot of work by hand. Work
keeps them well. They are often surprising combinations of

carpenters, paper-hangers, painters, and plumbers, as well as clam-diggers. They make their own dories and reach-boats at home still, as their fathers made their schooners and brigs. They build them in the barn in Winter; the boats grow bigger as the cows eat down the haymows; the women steam the ribs, and sons and daughters hold against their father as he drives home the bolts. And glory be! These boat-builders sail their own boats, keep their own hours, are their own bosses, take no man's orders but their own. They are cranky independents who employ themselves, trust nobody's judgment but their own, believe in hard work, and thinking and education, too. They speak in proverbs, they tell stories, and find time to whittle boats for little boys. Every so often a lobsterman fathers a daughter who paints or sings, or a son who draws pictures well, or at least a lawyer, a doctor, and a railroad president in one batch of children. They are not put out by anybody with airs or wealth. They judge a man by what he does and not what he has. They believe in the uncommon common men who have built up our country westward, state by state, and made America the model for democracies everywhere and the hope of the future.

Democracy is a word of dubious meaning nowadays. But Maine citizens are about what we used to mean by the word. They are people who follow many trades along lakes and bays like Norwegian fiords, men of wide reading and solid thinking, as well as artisans and hewers of wood.

The State of Maine is a state of making one's living off the country still, in the pioneer pattern of resourcefulness, piecening out the corn and beans with venison and fish. It is a state, mostly farms and villages or small towns, flourishing on old American resourcefulness which metropolitan Summer people come far to see and admire. It is like seeing Thomas Jefferson and Ben Franklin still alive, running boats and fishing.

Maine is a state, I claim, of being American.

There are more people in the graveyards than in the neat white houses and big barns and little boats. But maybe it is a good thing to have one's resourceful ancestors keeping an eye on a man from a marble monument on a hill. We don't get ahead much in population, but we hold our own. In humor and laughter as in numbers.

"Say," said the Summer visitor, "doesn't your town ever grow any bigger?"

"Well, would you believe it, marm, every time another boy is born around here, another young man leaves for Boston."

We still raise fair potatoes where our grandfathers raised theirs, build our lobster boats in the coves where our great-grandfathers built the ships that circled the world. We still go on begetting children who grow up and remain themselves and refuse to become the automatons that high-paid uplifters and the eye-servants of the state want men to be. We still make out with what little we have and stick to our own ideas of the Good.

Maine is really the state of being oneself.

It is a good state to act as usher of the sun each morning to other states, a fine rooster to wake up America to work.

Maine is a good state to have to look at when the world is in the sorry state of becoming enslaved to the state as it is just now.

Perhaps Arnold Toynbee ought to come Down East and see us some Summer.